T0004319

A
VERY
VEGAN
CHRISTMAS

A
VERY
VEGAN
CHRISTMAS

Plant-based recipes for celebrating in style

SAM DIXON

hamlyn

Contents

Introduction

Christmas was once very restricting for vegan home cooks, but nowadays with more and more people wanting to explore plant-based fare, food stores and suppliers stock a wealth of alternatives to the usual meat, fish and dairy ingredients. This collection of specially devised recipes elevates and celebrates the rich variety of seasonal vegetables and fruits, nuts and seeds, beans and lentils, and grains and pasta available to ensure you enjoy all the luxury and decadence that the holiday season affords.

Every aspect of Christmas cooking is covered, from nibbles to tipples through to centrepiece mains and complementary sides, showstopper desserts and bakes and even inventive ideas for leftovers. You can choose from plant-based twists on some festive classics that are equally if not more delicious than the originals, or dishes that offer an exciting departure from the traditional or something refreshingly unexpected yet just as perfect for your celebratory meal. There are also easy recipes for party food so you can fill a whole table with delicious treats and cater for a crowd – including any avid meat-eaters, who are guaranteed to be won over by the vegan canapés!

Many of these recipes can be prepped ahead, taking the stress out of cooking and giving you more time to spend with family and friends on the day. Just make sure to free up enough space in the freezer (it's an opportune moment to review your freezer contents in any case) and have some freezer-safe lidded containers in readiness. Some of the recipes in the Leftovers chapter make creative use of surpluses from the main and side dishes in the book, which means you can cook up two-in-one meals without much extra effort involved. The Baking chapter features recipes that make wonderful homemade foodie gifts or are ideal for filling up the cookie jar to keep hungry houseguests satisfied, or provide fun activity during the lull between Christmas and New Year.

With this array of impressive recipes, imaginative ideas and invaluable inspiration to draw on for the whole festive period, you're sure to have yourself A Very (Merry) Vegan Christmas!

CHAPTER 1

Party Food

An easy cocktail to whip up for groups, this is a lot more vibrant in colour than the classic version and is sure to set the fun party mood! Using double the quantity of pomegranate juice to vermouth makes it slightly sweeter too. Weighing the liquids in a jug is a really easy way to measure them.

Pomegranate Negroni

SERVES 6

150 g (5 oz) gin
150 g (5 oz) Campari
100 g (3½ oz) pomegranate
  juice
50 g (2 oz) sweet vermouth
ice
100 g (3½ oz) pomegranate
  seeds, to garnish

Set a large jug on a weighing scale and reset it to 0, then weigh in all the liquid ingredients.

Add some ice and give the mixture a really good stir.

Fill 6 tumblers with lots of ice or add one giant cube to each. Divide the cocktail between the glasses, garnish with the pomegranate seeds and serve immediately!

Creamy and lightly spiced, this alternative to the Christmas classic eggnog is lighter and easier to whip up in a hurry. For added convenience, it can be made the day before and the alcohol stirred through just before serving, if using.

Coco-nog

400 ml (14 oz) can coconut milk

500 ml (17 fl oz) dairy-free milk of your choice, but preferably oat or almond

75 g (3 oz) maple syrup, or more to taste

1 teaspoon vanilla extract

½ teaspoon ground cinnamon

¼ teaspoon freshly grated nutmeg, plus extra for dusting

pinch of ground cardamom

pinch of salt

2 tablespoons bourbon (optional)

2 tablespoons white rum (optional)

ice, to serve (optional)

Blitz together all the ingredients in a blender until thick and foamy.

Chill in the refrigerator, then pour over ice in glasses.

Alternatively, gently heat in a saucepan until warm, adding a little more maple syrup if you prefer it sweeter, then pour into mugs.

Grate a little nutmeg over the top of the drinks before serving.

Quick and easy to make, these flavoured nuts are the perfect accompaniment to a festive beverage. You can use any nut you like, and feel free to swap out the chilli and rosemary for other spices and seasonings you prefer. They can be prepared up to a week ahead as long as they are stored in an airtight container.

Roasted Spicy & Salty Almonds

SERVES 8

300 g (10 oz) whole almonds, skins on
2 tablespoons olive oil
1 teaspoon sea salt flakes
½ teaspoon chilli flakes
leaves from 3 rosemary sprigs, very roughly chopped
pinch of pepper

Preheat the oven to 180°C (350°F), Gas Mark 4, and line a baking tray with nonstick baking paper.

Toss the almonds with all the remaining ingredients and spread out on the lined tray.

Roast for 15–20 minutes. Remove from the oven and let the nuts cool completely before serving in little bowls.

This is a great dip for crudités or spread for crackers – seeded crackers make a perfect pairing, such as the Seedy Rosemary Crackers (see page 117). Just put the paté in a bowl in the middle of all the delicious accompaniments you want to offer and let your guests dig in.

Lemony Artichoke Pâté

SERVES 8–10

200 g (7 oz) grilled
   marinated artichokes
   hearts from a jar, drained
½ × 400 g (13 oz) can
   cannellini beans, drained
   and rinsed
2 garlic cloves, finely
   chopped
2 tablespoons olive oil, plus
   extra for drizzling
finely grated zest and juice of
   1 lemon
50 g (2 oz) vegan yogurt
50 g (2 oz) toasted pine nuts
salt and pepper

Blend together all the ingredients, except 15 g (½ oz) of the toasted pine nuts and seasoning, in a food processor until the mixture is the desired texture, smooth or coarse, depending on your preference. Season to taste with salt and pepper.

Transfer to a serving bowl, then drizzle with olive oil, top with a little more salt and pepper and sprinkle with the remaining toasted pine nuts before serving.

It wouldn't be a celebration without blinis. For an alternative vegan topping to the usual smoked salmon and soured cream, try this fresh minty pea combo.

Buckwheat Blinis with Pea Purée & Pickled Radishes

SERVES 8–10

Pickled radishes

50 ml (2 fl oz) vegan white
   wine vinegar
pinch of sugar
pinch of salt
100 g (3½ oz) radishes,
   quartered if small, or cut
   into 6 or 8 if large

Blinis

150 g (5 oz) buckwheat flour
50 g (2 oz) plain flour
2 teaspoons baking powder
½ teaspoon bicarbonate
   of soda
pinch of salt
2 teaspoons caster sugar
250 ml (8 fl oz) oat milk
vegetable oil, for frying

Pea purée

200 g (7 oz) frozen peas
1 garlic clove, peeled but
   kept whole
30 g (1 oz) vegan butter
1 tablespoon chopped
   mint leaves
pinch of salt and pepper

First make the pickled radishes. Heat the vinegar in a saucepan with the sugar and salt, stirring until they both dissolve. Pour over the radishes in a non-reactive bowl, pushing them down until coated and submerged in the vinegar, then set aside for at least 30 minutes.

Meanwhile, for the blinis, whisk together all the dry ingredients in a bowl. Make a well in the centre, pour in the oat milk and gradually whisk into the dry ingredients until all incorporated and you have a smooth batter. Cover with a clean tea towel and let the batter rest for 30 minutes.

For the pea purée, cook the peas along with the garlic clove in a saucepan of boiling water for 2 minutes. Drain and return to the pan with the vegan butter, mint and salt and pepper, then blitz with a stick blender or in a food processor until fairly smooth but retaining a bit of texture.

Once the blini batter has rested, heat a little drizzle of vegetable oil in a large frying pan, add as many separate teaspoonfuls of the batter as you can fit in the pan, spaced apart, and cook over a medium heat until bubbles form on the surface. Then flip over and cook until golden brown on both sides. Remove and place on a large baking tray.

When ready to serve, place a spoonful of pea purée on each blini and top with the pink pickled radishes.

This sushi is colourful, fresh and easy to make in a large batch for a big gathering. It can also be prepared the day before and stored in the refrigerator until ready to serve for convenience, and any leftovers are ideal for lunch the next day.

Vibrant Vegetable Sushi with Sriracha Mayo

SERVES 4–8

400 g (13 oz) sushi rice

2 tablespoons rice vinegar

1 tablespoon mirin

2 teaspoons salt

4 nori sheets

2 large carrots, peeled and grated or cut into matchsticks

¼ red cabbage, about 150 g (5 oz), finely shredded

1 cucumber, cut into matchsticks

Sriracha mayo

200 g (7 oz) vegan mayonnaise

4 tablespoons Sriracha

To serve

50 g (2 oz) shop-bought crispy fried shallots

30 g (1 oz) toasted sesame seeds

Cook the rice according to the packet instructions, then stir in the rice vinegar, mirin and salt and let it cool completely.

Meanwhile, mix together the ingredients for the Sriracha mayo in a small bowl.

Once the rice is cool, lay a nori sheet preferably on a bamboo rolling mat or, if you don't have one, a clean tea towel, with one shorter side nearest to you.

Divide the rice into 4 portions, then spread one portion evenly over the nori sheet, leaving a 2 cm (¾ inch) clear border along the shorter side furthest from you. Arrange one-quarter of each of the vegetables in a single row 2.5 cm (1 inch) from the nearer shorter side. With the help of the bamboo mat or tea towel, roll up the sushi tightly from the nearer shorter side, making sure the vegetables are firmly packed in. Brush the nori border with a little water and press against the roll to seal. Repeat with the remaining nori sheets and vegetables.

Using a sharp knife, slice the rolls into rounds and line up on a serving plate, standing on their sides if possible. Pipe the Sriracha mayo on the top of the sushi rolls using a disposable piping bag with the tip snipped off to make a small piping hole, or simply spoon it on, then scatter over the crispy fried shallots and toasted sesame seeds and serve.

Inspired by rösti, these crispy little cakes featuring grated raw beetroot instead of potato make for a great bite-sized nibble at a party, although you could form the beetroot batter into larger cakes for breakfast or brunch instead if preferred. The horseradish soured cream delivers a feisty flavour kick.

Beetroot & Caraway Cakes with Horseradish Soured Cream

SERVES 6–8

3 large beetroot (about 350 g/
  11½ oz), peeled and grated
1 red onion, grated
1 tablespoon caraway seeds
2 garlic cloves, crushed
handful of flat leaf parsley
  leaves, chopped
2 tablespoons plain flour
2 tablespoons olive oil
salt and pepper
handful of chives, snipped,
  to garnish

Horseradish soured cream
6 tablespoons vegan soured
  cream
3 tablespoons horseradish

Put the grated beetroot and onion into a bowl along with the caraway seeds, garlic, parsley, flour and some salt and pepper and mix together. Then using your hands, scrunch the mixture together until the moisture from the beetroot and the onion combines with the flour to make a binding batter.

Heat the olive oil in a large frying pan. Add as many separate tablespoonfuls of the beetroot batter as you can fit in the pan, spaced well apart, and flatten gently with the back of the spoon into mini cakes. Fry over a medium heat for 2 minutes until golden on the underside, then flip over and cook the other side until golden. Transfer the cooked cakes to a tray and fry the rest of the batter.

While the cakes are frying, mix together the ingredients for the horseradish soured cream in a small bowl.

Once cooked, leave the beetroot cakes to cool, then serve topped with the horseradish soured cream, garnished with the snipped chives.

When cooked and marinated in this way, watermelon becomes wonderfully savoury, almost like tuna tartare. Scooped up on crispy wonton wrappers, it makes a really yummy canapé. You can prepare and leave the watermelon to marinate in the refrigerator the day before the party.

Watermelon Tartare & Crispy Wontons

SERVES 6

watermelon, about 2 kg (4 lb), peeled, deseeded and cut into 1.5 cm (¾ inch) cubes
3 tablespoons light soy sauce
1 tablespoon sesame oil
2 spring onions, finely chopped
1 garlic clove, crushed
pinch of pepper
1 tablespoon toasted sesame seeds
500 ml (17 fl oz) vegetable oil
1 pack of wonton wrappers, roughly 20 sheets, cut diagonally in half into triangles

Cook the watermelon cubes in a large frying pan, in batches if necessary, over a medium heat without any oil until they release their excess liquid, then continue cooking until it evaporates and the pan is dry again.

Transfer the watermelon to a bowl and gently mix in the soy sauce, sesame oil, spring onions, garlic, pepper and sesame seeds. Cover and leave to marinate in the refrigerator for at least 1 hour.

Heat the vegetable oil in a large, deep heavy-based saucepan or deep-fat fryer (make sure there is at least 5 cm/2 inches between the surface of the oil and the top of the pan) to 180°C (350°F): add a tiny piece of wonton wrapper to the hot oil, and if it sizzles, the oil is ready.

Fry the wonton triangles in batches. Remove and drain on a plate lined with kitchen paper.

When ready to serve, put the watermelon tartare into a serving bowl in the middle of a plate and arrange the wonton triangles around the bowl.

These croquettes have great balance of flavour and texture. You can make them a day in advance and keep refrigerated until ready to fry.

Curried Parsnip Croquettes   SERVES 4–6

500 g (1 lb) parsnips, peeled
   and cut into chunks
1.5 litres (2 ½ pints)
   vegetable oil, for
   deep-frying
mango chutney, to serve
   (optional)

Sauce
50 g (2 oz) vegan butter
70 g (2¾ oz) plain flour
300 ml (½ pint) dairy-free
   milk
1 teaspoon Dijon mustard
1 tablespoon curry powder
½ teaspoon ground turmeric
pinch of chilli powder
salt and pepper

Coating
75 g (3 oz) plain flour
75 g (3 oz) dairy-free milk
100 g (3½ oz) panko
   breadcrumbs

Cook the parsnips in a saucepan of boiling water or steam for about 10–15 minutes until tender, then drain and cool.

To make the sauce, melt the vegan butter in a medium-sized saucepan over a medium heat, stir in the flour until you have a smooth paste and cook for 1 minute, stirring constantly. Gradually add the milk, and cook until the sauce thickens. Stir in the mustard and spices, and season to taste. Scrape the sauce into a bowl, let it cool and cover with clingfilm.

Blend the cooled parsnips in a food processor until fairly smooth, then stir into the cooled sauce, re-cover and refrigerate for 1–2 hours.

To coat the croquettes, put the flour, milk and panko breadcrumbs in 3 separate bowls. Scoop a heaped tablespoon of the parsnip mixture and roughly shape into a croquette. Lightly coat with the flour, then dip into the milk and then roll in the panko. Place the finished croquette on a baking tray. Repeat with the remaining mixture. Chill the croquettes in the refrigerator for at least 30 minutes, or overnight.

Heat the oil in a large, deep heavy-based saucepan or deep-fat fryer (make sure there is at least 5 cm/2 inches between the surface of the oil and the top of the pan) to 180°C (350°F): add a few breadcrumbs to the oil, and if they sizzle, the oil is ready.

Fry the croquettes in batches of 4–5 for about 2–3 minutes, or until golden brown. Remove and drain on a baking tray lined with kitchen paper, then let them cool for 2 minutes before serving with mango chutney, if preferred.

Crunchy, sticky, spicy, saucy – what more could you want in a party food? Be sure to have lots of napkins on hand, or even finger bowls of water, as this is a deliciously messy treat for your guests to get stuck into.

Crispy Fried Cauliflower in Korean Chilli Sauce

SERVES 6–8

60 g (2¼ oz) tapioca flour or rice flour for the batter, plus 125 g (4 oz) for coating
40 g (1½ oz) plain flour
½ teaspoon baking powder
½ teaspoon salt
large pinch of pepper
2 small cauliflowers, broken into small-sized florets and leaves
40 ml (1½ fl oz) ice-cold water
4 teaspoons white vinegar
1 litre (1¾ pints) vegetable oil, for deep-frying

Sauce
100 g (3½ oz) soft light brown sugar
60 g (2¼ oz) gochujang
60 g (2¼ oz) tomato ketchup
60 g (2¼ oz) Sriracha
100 ml (3½ fl oz) rice vinegar
2 tablespoons sesame oil
½ teaspoon garlic powder

Whisk together the 60 g (2¼ oz) tapioca or rice flour and the plain flour, baking powder, salt and pepper in a large bowl. Add the cauliflower florets and leaves and mix until well combined. Pour over the measured ice-cold water and vinegar and mix together to make a batter that coats the cauliflower florets well. If the batter is too thick, add a little more water.

Put the remaining tapioca or rice flour for coating in a separate bowl. Shake the excess batter off each floret in turn, then lightly coat in the flour and place on a wire rack set over a baking tray to air-dry for 10 minutes.

Heat the oil in a large, deep heavy-based saucepan or deep-fat fryer (make sure there is at least 5 cm/2 inches between the surface of the oil and the top of the pan) to 180°C (350°F): add a small amount of the batter to the oil, and if it sizzles, then the oil is ready.

While the oil is heating, put all the ingredients for the sauce in a small saucepan and stir together over a medium heat until the mixture starts bubbling and thickens. Remove from the heat.

recipe continues overleaf

To garnish

**2 tablespoons toasted
   mixed black and white
   sesame seeds**

2 spring onions, finely sliced

Fry the cauliflower florets and leaves in batches of 4–5 for 2–3 minutes, or until golden brown and crispy. Remove and drain on the cleaned wire rack set over the tray.

Once all the cauliflower are fried, add to a large bowl with the sauce and toss until they are fully coated. Sprinkle over the sesame seeds and spring onions and serve immediately.

Gyoza are surprisingly straightforward to make using shop-bought wrappers available in the freezer section of South East Asian food stores. You can find lots of great tutorials online on how to fold and seal the filling inside the wrappers, or simply seal the wrappers flat to make things super easy! They can be made a day in advance and refrigerated, or frozen for up to 2 months, before frying for an additional 2 minutes to ensure they are fully cooked. Perfect for a party, just put them out with little bowls of dipping sauces and chopsticks so that everyone can help themselves.

Sprout, Carrot & Tofu Gyoza SERVES 6–8

2 tablespoons sesame oil, plus extra for frying

150 g (5 oz) Brussels sprouts, thinly sliced

2 carrots, peeled and grated

4 garlic cloves, very finely chopped

thumb-sized piece of fresh root ginger, peeled and grated

4 spring onions, roughly chopped

50 g (2 oz) water chestnuts, finely chopped

200 g (7 oz) silken tofu

1 tablespoon light soy sauce

1 tablespoon Shaoxing rice wine

large pinch of pepper

25–30 shop-bought frozen gyoza wrappers, defrosted

crispy chilli oil, sweet chilli sauce and/or hoisin sauce, to serve

Heat 2 tablespoons sesame oil in a large frying pan and sauté the sprouts and carrots over a medium heat for 5 minutes until the vegetables soften. Stir in the garlic, ginger, spring onions and water chestnuts and cook for another 2 minutes. Then add the silken tofu, soy sauce, rice wine and pepper, stirring and breaking up the tofu with the back of the spoon. Remove from the heat and let the mixture cool completely in the pan.

Line a baking tray with nonstick baking paper.

Lay a gyoza wrapper in the palm of your hand and place a teaspoon of the filling in the centre. Dip a finger in water and dampen the edges of the wrapper, then fold the wrapper in half over the filling into a semicircle. Pinch the edges together at the midpoint, then use your thumb and index finger to make a series of pleats in the front layer of the semicircle, working from the midpoint to the right and then the midpoint to the left, pressing the pleats firmly against the back layer to seal. Repeat with the rest of the filling and wrappers.

recipe continues overleaf

Place the gyoza on the lined tray, cover and refrigerate if you are making up to a day ahead, or open-freeze and then, once frozen, transfer to a freezer bag or freezer-safe container with a lid.

When you are ready to cook, heat a good drizzle of sesame oil in a large frying pan over a medium heat. Add as many gyoza as will comfortably fit into the pan and fry for 5 minutes without moving them until nice and crispy on the underside, then pour in enough water to reach halfway up the gyoza, cover the pan with a lid and cook for 7 minutes, or until the water has completely evaporated.

Arrange the gyoza on a serving plate with whatever dipping sauces you fancy in little bowls alongside.

Drawing inspiration from Indian onion bhajis and vegetable pakoras, these lightly spiced and crispy little balls, served in a big pile, are sure to be quickly devoured.

Courgette, Carrot & Red Onion Spiced Fritters

SERVES 6–8

2 red onions, grated
1 courgette, grated
1 carrot, peeled and grated
1 green chilli, deseeded and finely chopped
100 g (3½ oz) gram (besan/ chickpea) flour
2 teaspoons ground coriander
1 teaspoon ground cumin
½ teaspoon chilli powder
½ teaspoon ground turmeric
1 teaspoon salt
1 litre (1¾ pints) vegetable oil, for deep-frying
vegan raita, to serve (optional)

Put all the ingredients, except the oil, into a large bowl and mix together. Then using your hands, scrunch the mixture together until the moisture from the vegetables combines with the flour to make a nice, thick batter. Add a little water, if necessary, to help bind the mixture, but you don't want it to be loose.

Heat the oil in a large, deep heavy-based saucepan or deep-fat fryer (make sure there is at least 5 cm/2 inches between the surface of the oil and the top of the pan) to 180°C (350°F): add a little of the mixture to the hot oil, and if it sizzles, the oil is ready.

Using 2 tablespoons, shape the mixture into balls. Drop carefully into the hot oil and fry in batches of 4–5 for 2–3 minutes, or until golden brown all over, turning over halfway through. Remove and drain on a baking tray lined with kitchen paper. Pile on to a plate and serve immediately with vegan raita, if preferred.

CHAPTER 2

Mains

This dish has the flavours of the classic Greek spinach pie spanakopita but uses ready-made shortcrust pastry instead of filo and is formed into the shape of a wreath for a perfect Christmas table centrepiece.

Spinach & Apricot Wreath

SERVES 6

2 tablespoons olive oil

2 onions, finely diced

4 garlic cloves, very finely chopped

250 g (8 oz) spinach leaves, wilted, drained and squeezed of excess moisture (see page 49)

50 g (2 oz) toasted pine nuts

handful of dill, chopped, plus extra fronds to garnish

handful of flat leaf parsley, chopped

finely grated zest of 1 lemon

50 g (2 oz) ready-to-eat dried apricots, roughly chopped

200 g (7 oz) silken tofu

500 g (1 lb) ready-made vegan shortcrust pastry

plain flour, for dusting

50 ml (2 fl oz) oat milk

50 g (2 oz) mixed black and white sesame seeds

salt and pepper

Heat the olive oil in a large frying pan and sauté the onions with the garlic over a medium heat for about 6 minutes until softened.

Stir in the wilted spinach and cook until any excess water evaporates. Then add the toasted pine nuts, herbs, lemon zest, apricots and tofu, season to taste with salt and pepper and mix together. Remove from the heat and let the mixture cool.

Preheat the oven to 200°C (400°F), Gas Mark 6. Line a large baking sheet with nonstick baking paper.

Roll out the pastry on a lightly floured work surface to a rectangle about 20 × 60 cm (8 × 24 inches). With one longer side nearest to you, spread the spinach mixture evenly over the pastry, leaving a 1.5 cm (¾ inch) clear border along both longer sides and a 2.5 cm (1 inch) clear border along both shorter sides. Roll up the pastry from the longer side nearest to you in a long sausage shape, then brush the opposite longer pastry border with a little water and press to seal. Place seam-side down and curve into a ring, then pinch the ends together to seal.

Slice the outer side of the ring into sausage-roll-sized sections, leaving the inner side intact so that it makes a neat wreath-like shape. Carefully transfer the wreath to the lined tray, brush all over with the oat milk and sprinkle over the sesame seeds. Bake for 45 minutes until golden brown. Remove from the oven and let the wreath cool for 10 minutes, then garnish with extra dill fronds, slice and serve.

If you want something a bit different as your Christmas main dish,
this make-ahead aubergine terrine will fit the bill perfectly with a
variety of seasonal accompaniments served alongside.

Aubergine Terrine

4 large aubergines, cut
   lengthways into about
   5 mm (¼ inch) thick slices
2 tablespoons olive oil
300 g (10 oz) vegan cream
   cheese
1 tablespoon vegan
   mayonnaise
1 tablespoon oat milk
1 garlic clove, crushed
2 roasted red peppers from
   a jar, drained and sliced
salt and pepper

Lay the aubergine slices on a chopping board, sprinkle with salt and leave for 10 minutes for the excess liquid to be released.

Meanwhile, preheat the grill to high.

Pat the aubergine slices dry with kitchen paper or a clean tea towel. Arrange them on baking trays, drizzle over the olive oil and season with pepper, then place under the hot grill for about 6 minutes, turning over halfway through cooking, or until nicely charred on both sides.

Mix together the vegan cream cheese and mayonnaise, oat milk and garlic in a bowl, and season to taste with salt and pepper.

Line a 1 kg (2 lb) loaf tin with a large piece of clingfilm so that there is plenty of excess clingfilm overlapping the sides. Lay a single layer of aubergine slices in the base of the tin, followed by a thin layer of the vegan cream cheese mixture, then a layer of roasted red pepper slices and another thin layer of the vegan cream cheese mixture. Repeat the layers, finishing with a final layer of aubergine on top, then cover the surface with the excess clingfilm.

Press down gently so that everything is firmly packed into the loaf tin, then chill in the refrigerator for 6 hours, or overnight.

When ready to serve, unwrap, gently unmould on to a plate and cut into thick slices.

An impressive dome-shaped pie, this is just as appealing on the inside with its colourful layered filling. It's also very tasty eaten cold out of the refrigerator the next day, should there be any leftovers.

Sweet Potato & Beetroot Pithivier

SERVES 6

250 g (8 oz) sweet potato, peeled and cubed

200 g (7 oz) beetroot, peeled and cubed

olive oil

1 teaspoon chilli flakes

leaves from 4 thyme sprigs

2 onions, thinly sliced

3 garlic cloves, very finely chopped

200 g (7 oz) cavolo nero, stalks discarded, leaves torn into small pieces

150 g (5 oz) silken tofu

50 ml (2 fl oz) vegan vegetable stock

1 tablespoon nutritional yeast

500 g (1 lb) ready-made vegan puff pastry

plain flour, for dusting

50 ml (2 fl oz) oat milk

salt and pepper

Preheat the oven to 200°C (400°F), Gas Mark 6.

Spread out the sweet potato and beetroot cubes separately on 2 baking trays. Drizzle both with olive oil and season with salt and pepper, then sprinkle half the chilli flakes and thyme leaves over each. Roast for about 30 minutes, or until tender. Remove from the oven and let the vegetables cool.

Heat 2 tablespoons olive oil in a large frying pan and sauté the onions over a medium heat for about 10 minutes until caramelized, then season with salt and pepper and transfer to a small bowl to cool.

Add a little more oil to the pan and sauté the garlic for 2 minutes, then add the cavolo nero and cook until just starting to wilt. Remove from the heat.

Blend together the tofu, stock and nutritional yeast in a blender, then stir into the cavolo nero and season to taste with salt and pepper.

Line a large baking tray with nonstick baking paper. Cut the puff pastry into 2 pieces, one slightly larger than the other. Roll out the smaller piece of pastry on a lightly floured work surface into a circle about 23 cm (9 inch) in diameter (you can cut around a cake tin or pie dish to make a perfect circle

recipe continues overleaf

if you like). Place on the lined tray and refrigerate while you roll out the other piece of pastry into a larger circle, at least 25 cm (10 inches) in diameter.

Dust the smaller pastry circle with flour, then spread over the caramelized onions evenly, leaving a 1.5 cm (¾ inch) clear border around the edge. Then add a layer of beetroot, followed by sweet potato and ending with the cavolo nero mixture. Brush the pastry border with a little oat milk, then lay over the larger circle of pastry, ensuring there is no air trapped inside, and press the edges together all the way round to seal. Then either crimp by pressing with a fork or pinching with your fingers.

Using a knife, lightly score lines from the centre down to the crimp and make a small hole in the centre for the steam to escape, then brush all over with the remaining oat milk and chill in the refrigerator for 30 minutes, or up to a day.

When ready to bake, preheat the oven to 200°C (400°F), Gas Mark 6. Bake for 45 minutes until golden brown and puffed up. Remove from the oven, let rest for 10 minutes and then cut into wedges to serve.

Sweet caramelized onions in a creamy tofu custard make a fittingly rich and satisfying filling for this short and nutty pastry case, and a delicious main dish for the festive table.

Caramelized Onion Tart

Spelt pastry

- 50 g (2 oz) walnuts
- 175 g (6 oz) spelt flour, plus extra for dusting
- pinch of salt
- 125 g (4 oz) vegan butter, chilled and cubed, plus extra for greasing
- leaves from 2 thyme sprigs
- 1–2 tablespoons ice-cold water

Filling

- 2 tablespoons olive oil, plus extra for roasting
- 5 medium onions, halved widthways
- 4 thyme sprigs, leaves stripped from 2 sprigs
- 300 g (10 oz) silken tofu
- 200 ml (7 fl oz) dairy-free milk
- 2 tablespoons nutritional yeast
- 6 garlic cloves, left whole with skin on
- salt and pepper

First make the pastry. Pulse the walnuts in a food processor until fairly finely ground. Add the flour, salt, vegan butter and thyme leaves from 2 sprigs and pulse until the mixture resembles coarse breadcrumbs. Then gradually add the measured ice-cold water, pulsing until the mixture starts coming together into a dough.

Form the dough into a disc, wrap closely and chill in the refrigerator for at least 30 minutes.

For the filling, heat the olive oil in a large frying pan, add the onions, cut-side down, and cook over a medium heat for about 5–8 minutes until lightly browned. Transfer to a plate. Fry the whole thyme sprigs in the remaining oil, then set aside to cool.

Blend together the tofu, dairy-free milk and nutritional yeast in a blender until completely smooth, then season to taste with salt and pepper.

When ready to bake, preheat the oven to 190°C (375°F), Gas Mark 5. Grease a 23 cm (9 inch) or similar-sized tart tin and lightly dust with flour.

Roll out the pastry on a lightly floured work surface into a circle large enough to line the tart tin. Lay the pastry out over the tin, press gently into the grooves and trim off any excess.

recipe continues overleaf

Prick the pastry base with a fork, cover and chill in the refrigerator for 30 minutes–1 hour.

Line the chilled tart case with nonstick baking paper, fill with baking beans or uncooked rice or pasta and bake for 15–20 minutes, or until the pastry is crisp and golden. On a separate tray, wrap the garlic cloves in a foil parcel, drizzle with oil and roast in the oven for the same duration.

Remove the tart case from the oven and lift out the paper and its contents. Arrange the onion halves, cut-side up, over the base of the tart case, carefully squeeze out the roasted garlic cloves onto the baked pastry case and then pour the tofu mixture in and around the onions. Place the tart case on a tray and bake for 40 minutes, or until the filling is firm and the onions are caramelized. Remove from the oven and let the tart cool in the tin for about 15 minutes, before breaking up the thyme sprigs and scattering over the top. Remove the tart from the tin and slice to serve.

Sweet and savoury lentils in a crisp filo wrapper complete with chive ties – this is a fun and festive way to serve your main dish.

Cranberry & Lentil Filo Christmas Crackers

MAKES 6

2 tablespoons olive oil, plus extra for brushing

2 onions, finely diced

1 celery stick, finely diced

1 carrot, peeled and finely diced

4 garlic cloves, very finely chopped

6 sage leaves, chopped

1 tablespoon tomato purée

1 teaspoon sweet smoked paprika

pinch of ground cloves

1 tablespoon light soy sauce

400 g (13 oz) ready-cooked Puy lentils

1 tablespoon cornflour

handful of flat leaf parsley leaves, chopped

200 g (7 oz) cranberry sauce

6 vegan filo pastry sheets, each about 48 × 25 cm (19 × 10 inches)

salt and pepper

12 chives, to garnish

Heat the olive oil in a large frying pan and sauté the onions, celery and carrot with the garlic over a medium heat for about 8 minutes until softened. Stir in the sage and cook for a minute or so, then add the tomato purée, spices, soy sauce, Puy lentils and cornflour, stir well and season to taste with salt and pepper. Remove from the heat and mix in the parsley and cranberry sauce.

Preheat the oven to 190°C (375°F), Gas Mark 5. Line 2 baking trays with nonstick baking paper.

Lay out a filo pastry sheet on a work surface and brush all over with olive oil, then repeat with another 2 filo sheets until you have 3 layers. Cut in half widthways to make 2 rectangles about 24 × 25 cm (9½ × 10 inches). Divide the lentil mixture into 6 equal portions. With one of the longer sides nearest to you, form a portion into a long sausage shape in the centre of each rectangle, leaving about a 6 cm (2½ inch) clear border at either end. Brush the opposite longer side of the pastry with olive oil, then roll up the pastry from the nearer longer side tightly around the filling and twist at either end like a Christmas cracker so that the excess pastry fans out slightly.

Repeat with the remaining filo sheets and lentil mixture until you have 6 crackers. Place 3 on each tray, seam-side down, brush all over with olive oil and bake for 20–30 minutes, or until the pastry is golden brown all over. Remove from the oven, and when ready to serve, tie a chive around either end of each cracker.

This truly is a mega centrepiece for your Christmas feast. Layers of soft, almost creamy vegetables are sandwiched between those of sweet and savoury nut roast for a wonderful contrast of flavour and texture as well as colour. It's easy to prep ahead too.

Rainbow Layered Nut Roast

SERVES 8

Sweet potato layer
625 g (1¼ lb) sweet potato, peeled and thinly sliced into half-moons
2 tablespoons olive oil
leaves from 3 thyme sprigs
1 teaspoon ground cumin
1 tablespoon maple syrup

Spinach layer
300 g (10 oz) spinach leaves
2 tablespoons olive oil
1 onion, finely diced
4 garlic cloves, very finely chopped
pinch of ground nutmeg

Beetroot hummus layer
300 g (10 oz) ready-cooked beetroot
400 g (13 oz) can chickpeas, drained and rinsed
1 garlic clove, very finely chopped
1 tablespoon lemon juice
2 tablespoons tahini
¼ teaspoon sweet smoked paprika
1–2 tablespoons olive oil, if needed

For the sweet potato layer, preheat the oven to 200°C (400°F), Gas Mark 6. Toss the sweet potato slices in the olive oil, thyme leaves, cumin, maple syrup and some salt and pepper. Spread out on a large baking tray and roast for 20 minutes, or until soft and just about to colour. Remove from the oven and let them cool.

Meanwhile, for the spinach layer, put the spinach into a large saucepan with a splash of water, cover with a lid and cook briefly over a low heat until wilted. Drain and squeeze out the excess moisture. Heat the olive oil in the pan and sauté the onion with the garlic over a medium heat for about 6 minutes until softened. Add the spinach, nutmeg and salt and pepper to taste, stir well and cook until any remaining liquid has evaporated. Remove from the heat and set aside.

For the beetroot hummus layer, blend together all the ingredients, except for the olive oil, in a food processor, seasoning to taste with salt and pepper. Then mix in just enough oil to moisten if the mixture is too dry – you don't want a loose consistency like a regular hummus, as it needs to hold its shape.

For the nut roast layer (ingredients overleaf), heat the olive oil in a large frying pan over a medium heat and cook the onions for about 8 minutes until slightly caramelized.

recipe continues overleaf

Nut roast layer

2 tablespoons olive oil, plus extra for greasing

4 red onions, finely diced

6 sage leaves, chopped

leaves from 1 rosemary sprig, chopped

2 tablespoons vegan red wine vinegar

2 tablespoons soft light brown sugar

750 g (1½ lb) mixed nuts

100 g (3½ oz) ready-cooked peeled chestnuts, roughly chopped

2 tablespoons dark soy sauce

2–3 tablespoons tahini

100 g (3½ oz) fresh white breadcrumbs

salt and pepper

Stir in the herbs, vinegar and sugar and cook for another 2 minutes until the vinegar evaporates and the sugar dissolves. Remove from the heat.

Pulse the mixed nuts and chestnuts in a food processor until mostly finely chopped but with a few coarse pieces for texture. The mixture should be soft but not mushy. Transfer to a large bowl, add the caramelized onions and the remaining ingredients, along with salt and pepper to taste, and mix until well combined and the mixture holds together if you squeeze some in your hand. If it doesn't, add a little more tahini.

Preheat the oven to 160°C (325°F), Gas Mark 3. Grease a 25 cm (10 inch) springform cake tin and line with nonstick baking paper. Divide the nut mixture into quarters. Spread one-quarter evenly over the base of the tin and press down. Repeat with the sweet potato slices, followed by another quarter of the nut mixture, then add the spinach and another quarter of the nut mixture, and lastly the beetroot hummus topped with the final quarter of nut mixture. Make sure everything is firmly pressed down, then bake for 40 minutes. Remove from the oven and leave to cool in the tin for 15 minutes before flipping out and slicing into wedges to serve.

Carrot and swede mash is a firm favourite side dish for a roast, so why not make it into the main event? For a nut-free version, simply substitute with ready-cooked brown or red lentils. You can use any leftovers in Nut Roast Wraps (see page 91).

Carrot, Swede & Parsnip Nut Roast

SERVES 6–8

3 large carrots, about 400 g (13 oz), peeled and cubed

300 g (10 oz) swede, peeled and cubed

500 g (1 lb) parsnips, peeled and cubed

olive oil

2 tablespoons finely chopped rosemary leaves

2 onions, finely diced

2 celery sticks, finely diced

4 garlic cloves, very finely chopped

2 tablespoons tomato purée

2 tablespoons light soy sauce

400 g (13 oz) can chickpeas, drained and rinsed

50 g (2 oz) fresh wholemeal breadcrumbs

100 g (3½ oz) pistachio nuts, roughly chopped

100 g (3½ oz) cashew nuts, roughly chopped

handful of flat leaf parsley, roughly chopped

20 g (¾ oz) pumpkin seeds

20 g (¾ oz) sunflower seeds

salt and pepper

Preheat the oven to 200°C (400°F), Gas Mark 6. Grease a 1 kg (2 lb) loaf tin and line with nonstick baking paper.

Put the carrot, swede and parsnip cubes into a large roasting tray and toss with a little olive oil, salt and pepper and the rosemary. Roast for about 30 minutes until the vegetables are cooked and a little crisp.

Meanwhile, heat 2 tablespoons of olive oil in a large frying pan and sauté the onions with the celery and garlic over a medium heat for about 6 minutes until softened. Stir in the tomato purée, soy sauce and chickpeas, remove from the heat and let the mixture cool.

Once the vegetables are roasted, mix with the chickpea mixture. Set aside half the mixture in a large bowl and pulse the other half with the breadcrumbs in a food processor until you have a slightly coarse purée. Mix with the unblended mixture, then stir through the nuts and parsley and season to taste with salt and pepper.

Press the mixture into the lined loaf tin and rough up the surface with a fork so that it will get extra crispy. Drizzle with a little olive oil, sprinkle over the seeds and bake for 45 minutes until golden brown. Remove from the oven and let the loaf cool in the tin for 10 minutes before removing from the tin and slicing to serve.

If you want an effortless festive showstopper, this is the recipe to go for, especially delicious served with the Mushroom & Onion Gravy (see page 79). But equally, you could make this any time you fancy a special yet easy meal.

Butternut Squash Stuffed with Puy Lentils, Walnuts & Cranberries

SERVES 4

1 large butternut squash, about 1 kg (2 lb)
olive oil
1 large onion, finely diced
4 garlic cloves, very finely chopped
1 tablespoon thyme leaves
6 sage leaves, finely chopped
200 g (7 oz) ready-cooked Puy lentils
100 g (3½ oz) walnuts, toasted and roughly chopped
50 g (2 oz) dried cranberries
salt and pepper
handful of flat leaf parsley, roughly chopped, to serve

Preheat the oven to 200°C (400°F), Gas Mark 6.

Cut the butternut squash in half lengthways, then scoop out the seeds and discard. Place the halves, cut-side up, on a baking tray, drizzle with olive oil and season with salt and pepper. Roast for 1 hour.

Meanwhile, heat 2 tablespoons olive oil in a large frying pan and sauté the onion with the garlic over a medium heat for about 6 minutes until softened. Stir in the herbs and cook for another 2 minutes. Season to taste with salt and pepper, then remove from the heat. Stir through the lentils, walnuts and cranberries.

When the squash is cooked, scoop a little of it out and add to the lentil mixture, then roughly mash so that it breaks down. Spoon the rest of the lentil mixture on to the slightly hollowed-out squash halves, drizzle a little more olive oil over and roast for another 10 minutes, just to allow the topping to crisp up. Scatter over the parsley and serve with your favourite sides.

A vegan take on the celebratory classic made with both fresh and dried mushrooms, the Marmite gives this dish an extra glossy and savoury finish.

Mushroom Wellington

15 g (½ oz) dried wild
  mushrooms
150 ml (¼ pint) boiling water
1 tablespoon olive oil
1 onion, finely diced
1 celery stick, finely diced
1 large carrot, peeled and
  finely diced
4 garlic cloves, very finely
  chopped
300 g (10 oz) oyster
  mushrooms, roughly
  chopped
leaves from 2 rosemary
  sprigs, roughly chopped
5 sage leaves, roughly chopped
1 tablespoon tomato purée
1 tablespoon light soy sauce
400 g (13 oz) can pinto
  beans, drained and rinsed
handful of flat leaf parsley
  leaves, chopped
50 g (2 oz) fresh white
  breadcrumbs
2 × 320 g (11 oz) ready-rolled
  vegan puff pastry sheets
250 g (8 oz) spinach
  leaves, wilted, drained
  and squeezed of excess
  moisture (see page 49)

Put the dried mushrooms into a heatproof bowl, pour over the measured boiling water and let them soak for 30 minutes.

Meanwhile, heat the olive oil in a large frying pan and sauté the onion, celery and carrot with the garlic over a medium heat for about 8 minutes until softened. Stir in the oyster mushrooms and herbs and cook for 5 minutes.

Once the dried mushrooms are rehydrated, drain, reserving the soaking liquid, and roughly chop, then add to the pan along with the soaking liquid, tomato purée and soy sauce and cook for 10 minutes until the liquid has almost all evaporated. Stir in the pinto beans, parsley and breadcrumbs, season to taste with salt and pepper and set aside to cool completely.

Preheat the oven to 190°C (375°F), Gas Mark 5. Line a large baking tray with nonstick baking paper and lay one puff pastry sheet on it. Spread one-third of the wilted spinach over the pastry, leaving a 2.5 cm (1 inch) clear border around the sides. Top with a layer of beetroot (see overleaf), then add the bean and mushroom mixture, slightly packing it into a large sausage shape with your hands dampened with water. Lastly cover with the remaining spinach.

Mix together the oat milk and Marmite in a small bowl, then brush on to the pastry border. Lay the other pastry

recipe continues overleaf

250 g (8 oz) ready-cooked
   beetroot, thinly sliced
50 ml (2 fl oz) oat milk
1 teaspoon Marmite
50 g (2 oz) nigella seeds
salt and pepper

sheet over the top, ensuring there is no air trapped, and press the edges together to seal. Then either crimp the edges by pressing with a fork or pinching with your fingers. Using a knife, lightly score a pattern in the top and make a few small holes for the steam to escape, then brush all over with the oat milk mixture and sprinkle over the nigella seeds.

Bake for 40 minutes, or until golden brown. Remove from the oven and let it cool for 10 minutes, then slice and serve.

Soft and sweet chilli-spiked pumpkin with crispy herby polenta cubes, this dish will be sure to wow your guests with its lovely balance of flavours and textures.

Crispy Polenta & Pumpkin

SERVES 4–6

1 pumpkin, about 1 kg (2 lb), peeled if the skin is tough, then halved, deseeded and cut into 1.5 cm (¾ inch) thick wedges
2 onions, cut into thin wedges
2 tablespoons olive oil
leaves from 4 thyme sprigs
1 teaspoon chilli flakes
salt and pepper

Polenta
500 ml (17 fl oz) vegan vegetable stock
150 g (5 oz) quick-cook polenta
1 tablespoon dried thyme
½ teaspoon ground nutmeg
50 g (2 oz) vegan butter
5 tablespoons vegetable oil, plus extra for greasing
8 sage leaves

First prepare the polenta. Line an 20 cm (8 inch) deep roasting tin or cake tin with nonstick baking paper and lightly brush vegetable oil all over the paper.

Bring the stock to the boil in a medium-sized saucepan, then pour in the polenta while stirring, along with the thyme. Cook, stirring constantly, for about 2 minutes, then season with the nutmeg and a little salt and pepper to taste. Remove the pan from the heat and mix in the vegan butter until melted and combined, then cover the pan with a lid and let the polenta rest for 5 minutes.

Pour the polenta into the prepared tray and spread out evenly. Set aside for about 20 minutes until cooled and set, while you get on with the pumpkin.

Preheat the oven to 200°C (400°F), Gas Mark 6. Line a baking tray with nonstick baking paper.

Spread the pumpkin and onion wedges out on the lined tray, drizzle all over with the olive oil and sprinkle with the thyme leaves, chilli flakes and a good pinch of salt and pepper. Roast for 30–40 minutes until the pumpkin is soft and slightly charred on the edges.

recipe continues overleaf

Meanwhile, once the polenta has set, heat the vegetable oil in a large frying pan. Roughly tear the polenta into 2.5 cm (1 inch) chunks and fry in batches for about 2 minutes, turning a few times, until golden brown and crunchy on all sides. Remove and drain on a large plate lined with kitchen paper. Fry the sage leaves in the remaining oil for a few seconds each side until they are beginning to brown. Remove and drain as before.

When the pumpkin is ready, toss it and the onions with the fried polenta cubes, transfer to a large platter and serve, topped with the crispy sage leaves.

Not only does salt baking lock in all the natural flavours of the ingredient within, it's also a lot of fun to crack into when placed in the middle of the table. With this treatment, the rustic-looking celeriac is elevated to something rather more sensational and celebratory.

Spiced Salt-baked Celeriac

SERVES 4

1 large celeriac, about
   1 kg (2 lb)
olive oil
1 tablespoon coriander seeds
1 teaspoon fennel seeds
1 teaspoon cumin seeds
pinch of chilli flakes
pinch of pepper
vegan butter, to serve
   (optional)

Salt dough
300 g (10 oz) plain flour,
   plus extra for dusting
175 g (6 oz) fine salt
2 tablespoons chopped
   rosemary leaves
2 tablespoons olive oil
150 ml (¼ pint) warm water

Scrub and wash the celeriac thoroughly, leaving the skin on, then trim the base so that it sits squarely.

Rub a little olive oil all over the celeriac, along with the spice seeds, chilli flakes and pepper so that they are evenly distributed. Set aside.

To make the salt dough, mix all the ingredients in a bowl until they come together into a dough, then knead the dough on a lightly floured work surface until smooth. Cover with a clean tea towel and let the dough rest for 20 minutes.

Preheat the oven to 180°C (350°F), Gas Mark 4. Line a baking tray with nonstick baking paper.

Roll out the dough on a lightly floured work surface until large enough to completely cover the celeriac. Place the celeriac in the middle and wrap the dough tightly around it, ensuring there is no air trapped inside. If there are any cracks in the dough, dip your finger in a little water and smooth over to seal. Place on the lined tray and bake for 2½ hours.

Remove from the oven and place in the middle of the table, crack open the top of the salt dough with a knife and scoop into the celeriac, then drizzle with a little olive oil or vegan butter and serve.

Based on the principle of the tarte Tatin, this puff pastry special with sweet caramelized leeks and crunchy walnuts looks as good as it tastes.

Leek & Walnut Upside-down Tart

SERVES 6

4 large leeks, trimmed and green tops discarded, cleaned and halved lengthways
2 tablespoons olive oil
leaves from 3 thyme sprigs
100 g (3½ oz) walnut pieces
320 g (11 oz) ready-rolled vegan puff pastry sheet
2 tablespoons soft light brown sugar
25 g (1 oz) vegan butter
2 tablespoons apple cider vinegar
salt and pepper

Preheat the oven to 200°C (400°F), Gas Mark 6.

Arrange the leeks in a large ovenproof dish, then drizzle with the olive oil, season with salt and pepper and scatter over the thyme leaves. Roast for about 20 minutes until soft and lightly coloured.

Meanwhile, heat a dry ovenproof frying pan about 20–23 cm (8–9 inches) in diameter over a medium heat and toast the walnuts lightly for about 3 minutes. Transfer to a plate and set aside.

Lay out the puff pastry on a clean work surface and cut out a rough circle about 2.5 cm (1 inch) larger in diameter than the frying pan.

When the leeks are done, heat the sugar, vegan butter and vinegar gently in the pan until the sugar dissolves, then remove from the heat. Scatter over the walnuts and arrange the roasted leeks on top of the caramel and nuts in a neat row. Lay the pastry circle over the top, tucking in the excess pastry around the edges. Prick all over with a fork and bake for about 25 minutes, or until the pastry is golden brown.

Wearing oven gloves, remove the pan from the oven and let the tart sit for a few minutes. Then place a plate slightly larger than the pan over the top of the pan and carefully invert together to turn the tart out on to the plate. Cut into wedges and serve.

CHAPTER 3

Sides

These are next-level roast potatoes, the polenta coating giving them an extra-crispy exterior. The soft, mellow-tasting roasted garlic makes a wonderful accompaniment.

Polenta & Rosemary Roast Potatoes

SERVES 4–6

150–200 ml (5–7 fl oz) vegetable oil

1.5 kg (3 lb) potatoes, such as King Edwards or Maris Piper, peeled and halved if small or quartered if large

3 tablespoons quick-cook polenta

leaves from 4 rosemary sprigs, roughly chopped

1 head of garlic, cloves separated and unpeeled

finely grated zest of 1 lemon

salt and pepper

Preheat the oven to 200°C (400°F), Gas Mark 6. Pour enough of the vegetable oil into a large roasting tray to cover the base liberally and put into the oven to heat up.

Meanwhile, parboil the potatoes in a large saucepan of salted boiling water for about 8 minutes until a fork just pushes into a potato – you don't want them overcooked and mushy. Drain and toss in the polenta along with some salt and pepper.

Once the oil is hot, remove the tray from the oven and carefully add the potatoes, rosemary and garlic cloves. Toss together well, add another seasoning of salt and pepper and drizzle over a little more oil if needed. Roast for 30–40 minutes until the potatoes are crispy on the underside, then turn over and roast for another 30–40 minutes until golden brown and crispy all over.

Remove from the oven and drain the potatoes on a baking tray lined with kitchen paper. Scatter over the lemon zest and serve, ensuring everyone gets a garlic clove or two for them to squeeze the gooey flesh out of the skins and smear all over their roast potatoes!

Cauliflower cheese's more sophisticated and dairy-free cousin, this creamy cabbage dish is delicious even on its own as a lunch option.

Creamy Hispi Cabbage

SERVES 4

1 hispi (sweetheart) cabbage,
  quartered lengthways
2 tablespoons vegan butter
2 tablespoons plain flour
475 ml (16 fl oz) oat milk or
  other dairy-free milk
1 teaspoon Dijon mustard
a few gratings of nutmeg
salt and pepper

Blanch the cabbage quarters in a large saucepan of salted boiling water for 2 minutes, then drain and let them steam dry while you make the sauce.

Melt the vegan butter in the same pan over a medium heat, stir in the flour until you have a smooth paste and cook for 1 minute or so, stirring constantly. Gradually add the dairy-free milk, continuing to stir constantly, and cook until the sauce is smooth and thickens enough to coat the back of the spoon. Stir in the mustard and nutmeg, and season to taste with salt and pepper. Remove from the heat.

Preheat the grill to high.

Line a baking tray with foil and lay the cabbage quarters on it. Spoon over the sauce, ensuring it penetrates the cabbage leaves and there is a thick layer on top. Place under the hot grill and cook until the cabbage is nicely charred and the sauce is brown and bubbling. Serve immediately.

This is a light alternative to roasted veg, featuring fresh raw winter vegetables dotted with spicy-sweet cashew nuts. The key to the slaw is in the preparation of the ingredients, as they need to be cut finely while retaining their crunch. For thinly slicing the sprouts and onion, use a mandoline if possible or, if you don't have one, a very sharp knife.

Winter Slaw

SERVES 6–8

125 g (4 oz) soya yogurt

60 g (2¼ oz) vegan
mayonnaise

juice of 1 lemon

1 tablespoon Dijon mustard

1 tablespoon maple syrup

500 g (1 lb) Brussels sprouts,
thinly sliced

3 carrots, peeled and cut into
matchsticks

1 red onion, thinly sliced

½ celeriac, peeled and cut
into matchsticks

handful of dill fronds,
roughly chopped

salt and pepper

Cashews

350 g (11½ oz) cashew nuts

2 tablespoons maple syrup

1 tablespoon olive oil

1 teaspoon ground turmeric

1 teaspoon ground cumin

1 teaspoon paprika

1 teaspoon salt

½ teaspoon pepper

First prepare the cashews. Preheat the oven to 200°C (400°F), Gas Mark 6. Line a baking tray with nonstick baking paper.

Toss the cashews with all the remaining ingredients in a bowl, then spread out on the lined tray and roast for 12 minutes. Remove from the oven and set aside to cool completely.

Mix together the soya yogurt, vegan mayonnaise, lemon juice, mustard and maple syrup in a large bowl, then season to taste with salt and pepper.

Add all the prepared vegetables with the dill and mix together thoroughly so that they are well coated in the dressing mixture.

Once the cashews are cooled, scatter over the slaw and serve.

You won't miss the cheese in this homage to cheesy leeks,
as the oaty topping provides plenty of satisfyingly savoury
flavour as well as contrastingly crunchy texture.

Leek & Oat Crumble SERVES 4–6

2 tablespoons olive oil

5 leeks, trimmed and green tops discarded, cleaned and sliced into 1.5 cm (¾ inch) thick rounds

2 garlic cloves, very finely chopped

leaves from 2 thyme sprigs

50 g (2 oz) vegan butter

50 g (2 oz) plain flour

200 ml (7 fl oz) oat milk

200 ml (7 fl oz) hot vegan vegetable stock

1 teaspoon mustard powder

pinch of grated nutmeg

salt and pepper

Crumble topping

50 g (2 oz) plain flour

50 g (2 oz) vegan butter, chilled and cubed

50 g (2 oz) porridge oats

1 tablespoon dried thyme

1 tablespoon nutritional yeast

pinch of salt and pepper

Heat the olive oil in a large frying pan and cook the leek rounds with the garlic and thyme leaves over a medium heat for about 5 minutes until they just start to soften. Transfer to a medium-sized ovenproof dish.

Melt the vegan butter in the same pan over a medium heat, stir in the flour until you have a smooth paste and cook for 1 minute or so, stirring constantly. Gradually add the oat milk and hot stock, continuing to stir constantly, and cook until the sauce is smooth and thickens. Stir in the mustard powder and nutmeg, and season to taste with salt and pepper. Pour the sauce over the leeks.

Preheat the oven to 200°C (400°F), Gas Mark 6.

For the crumble topping, put the flour into a bowl, add the vegan butter and rub in with your fingertips until the mixture resembles coarse breadcrumbs. Stir in the remaining ingredients and then gently clump together some of the mixture into fairly large lumps.

Scatter the crumble over the leeks and bake for about 20 minutes, or until the crumble is crisp and golden brown and the sauce is oozy. Serve immediately.

This simple and delicious way of preparing sprouts allows them to cook quickly and crisp up nicely, and the added garlic and sage really elevates the flavour.

Crispy Sage & Garlic Brussels Sprouts

SERVES 4–6

4 tablespoons olive oil

15 sage leaves, 8 left whole, 7 roughly chopped

5 garlic cloves, thinly sliced

1 kg (2 lb) Brussels sprouts, thinly sliced

salt and pepper

Heat the olive oil in a large frying pan, preferably with a lid, over a medium heat and fry the whole sage leaves for up to a minute, or until crisp. Remove and drain on a plate lined with kitchen paper.

Add the garlic with the chopped sage to the oil in the pan and cook for about 2 minutes until softened. Then add the sprouts and stir until they are well coated in the garlicky oil. Cover the pan with the lid and cook for about 5 minutes until the sprouts soften and turn bright green.

Season to taste with salt and pepper and serve topped with the whole crispy sage leaves.

This is the perfect recipe for when the oven is fully occupied with all the other Christmas dishes – caramelized carrots without the need for roasting. The maple syrup glaze gives them a lovely flavour and the pecans offer a pleasing nutty crunch.

Maple & Pecan Stove-top Carrots

SERVES 4–6

2 tablespoons olive oil
500 g (1 lb) carrots, peeled and sliced into 1.5 cm (¾ inch) rounds
200 ml (7 fl oz) hot vegan vegetable stock
3 thyme sprigs
2 tablespoons maple syrup
100 g (3½ oz) pecan nuts, toasted and roughly chopped
salt and pepper

Heat the olive oil in a large frying pan, preferably with a lid, and arrange the carrot rounds so that they are all sitting flat and fit snugly. Cover the pan with the lid, if it has one, and cook over a medium heat for 5 minutes, without stirring so that the carrots gain some colour on the underside.

Pour in the hot stock, add the thyme sprigs and season to taste with salt and pepper, then cook, uncovered, for about 10 minutes, or until the stock has evaporated.

Drizzle over the maple syrup and stir in, flipping the carrot slices over, then cook for another 5 minutes.

Give the carrots a final stir to ensure they are caramelized all over, before scattering over the toasted pecans and serving.

*This super-quick and easy side dish is a really delicious –
and nutritious – alternative to mashed potatoes. It's a handy
store-cupboard staple recipe to have in your repertoire.*

Garlicky White Bean Mash

SERVES 4–6

2 tablespoons olive oil, plus
    extra for drizzling
1 onion, finely diced
5 garlic cloves, very finely
    chopped
2 × 400 g (13 oz) cans butter
    or cannellini beans,
    drained and rinsed
juice of 1 lemon
100 ml (3½ fl oz) oat milk
a few gratings of nutmeg
salt and pepper

Heat the olive oil in a large saucepan and sauté the onion
with the garlic over a medium heat for 5 minutes until
softened and lightly coloured.

Add the beans and heat gently, then stir in the lemon juice
and the oat milk and heat through.

Blend the bean mixture with a stick blender or in a food
processor until smooth and creamy, or retain a bit of texture
if you prefer. Add the nutmeg and season to taste with salt
and pepper, then serve topped with a drizzle of olive oil.

The dried mushrooms give this gravy a rich and deep flavour – including their soaking liquid, which should always be added to the dish whenever you use rehydrated dried mushrooms. You can make and freeze this gravy several weeks ahead of time.

Mushroom & Onion Gravy

SERVES 6–8

30 g (1 oz) dried wild
    mushrooms
300 ml (½ pint) boiling
    water
1 tablespoon olive oil
3 red onions, finely sliced
1 heaped tablespoon
    plain flour
1 teaspoon miso paste
750 ml (1¼ pints) vegan
    vegetable stock
1 tablespoon dark soy sauce
pepper

Put the dried mushrooms into a large heatproof bowl, pour over the measured boiling water and let them soak for 30 minutes.

Meanwhile, heat the olive oil in a saucepan and sauté the onions over a medium heat for about 6–8 minutes until soft and caramelized.

Once the mushrooms are rehydrated, drain, reserving the soaking liquid, and roughly chop. Add the mushrooms to the pan and cook over a medium heat for 5 minutes.

Add the flour and miso paste and stir until the flour has coated the onions and mushrooms, then cook for another minute or so. Pour in the mushroom soaking liquid, stock and soy sauce, stirring as you go. Increase the heat a little and cook, continuing to stir constantly, until the gravy thickens. Season to taste with pepper. If you prefer a smooth, thicker gravy, blitz it with a stick blender or in a food processor. Serve hot, or leave to cool completely if freezing for future use.

This easy, tasty stuffing is not just for Christmas – add it to your
regular Sunday lunch menu to serve alongside your favourite mains.

Mushroom & Chestnut Stuffing

SERVES 4–6

2 tablespoons olive oil

2 leeks, trimmed, cleaned
and finely sliced

leaves from 3 thyme sprigs

6 sage leaves, roughly
chopped

250 g (8 oz) chestnut
mushrooms, roughly
chopped

250 g (8 oz) oyster
mushrooms, roughly
chopped

splash of vegan dry
white wine

4 garlic cloves, crushed

125 g (4 oz) sourdough
bread, crusts removed

200 g (7 oz) ready-cooked
peeled chestnuts

handful of flat leaf
parsley leaves

salt and pepper

Preheat the oven to 200°C (400°F), Gas Mark 6.

Heat the olive oil in a large frying pan and sauté the leeks
over a medium heat for about 6–8 minutes until softened.

Add the thyme and sage leaves, mushrooms, wine and garlic
and cook for about 5 minutes, or until the mushrooms have
softened. Remove from the heat.

Pulse the bread in a food processor until you have coarse
breadcrumbs. Add the mushroom mixture, chestnuts,
parsley and salt and pepper and pulse until the mixture just
comes together.

Transfer the stuffing mixture to a small ovenproof dish and
spread into an even layer. Bake for 35 minutes, or until crispy
and golden on top. Remove from the oven, spoon on to
plates and serve.

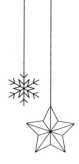

Inspired by the classic French dish pommes Anna, here Jerusalem artichokes are cooked in a mixture of vegan butter and olive oil. It's a lighter alternative to Dauphinoise, packed full of flavour from the nutty, earthy artichokes and garlicky oil.

Jerusalem Artichoke Cake with Rosemary & Garlic

SERVES 4–6

750 g (1½ lb) Jerusalem
    artichokes, scrubbed
juice of 1 lemon
50 ml (2 fl oz) olive oil
6 garlic cloves, thinly sliced
leaves from 4 rosemary
    sprigs
100 g (3½ oz) vegan butter
salt and pepper

Preheat the oven to 190°C (375°F), Gas Mark 5.

Thinly slice the Jerusalem artichokes with either a mandoline or a very sharp knife and sprinkle with the lemon juice to prevent discolouration.

Grease a large round ovenproof dish, about 23 cm (9 inches) in diameter, with some of the olive oil. Layer the dish with the artichoke slices, interspersed with the garlic, rosemary and salt and pepper, and dotting around small pieces of the vegan butter and drizzling over more olive oil, so that the ingredients are evenly distributed between the artichoke layers.

Once you have finished layering the artichoke slices, press the surface down gently with the palms of your hands, then add a final drizzle of olive oil and a seasoning of salt and pepper. Bake for 45 minutes, or until the artichokes are brown and crispy on top. Remove from the oven, cut the cake into wedges and serve.

A vibrant and flavourful side dish, this goes really well with the Aubergine Terrine (see page 38). But it's also good as a main dish for a midweek meal. You might not need all the dukkah, so store any left over in a little airtight jar for sprinkling over avocado on toast or hummus.

Roasted Cauliflower with Dukkah & Pomegranate Seeds

SERVES 4–6

1 large cauliflower, outer leaves discarded, inner leaves reserved and cauliflower broken into medium-sized florets
2 tablespoons olive oil, plus extra for drizzling
½ teaspoon ground turmeric
salt and pepper
100 g (3½ oz) pomegranate seeds
small handul of flat leaf parsley leaves, to serve

Dukkah
3 tablespoons sesame seeds
1 tablespoon coriander seeds
1 tablespoon fennel seeds
1 tablespoon cumin seeds
1 teaspoon chilli flakes
½ tablespoon sea salt flakes
½ teaspoon black pepper

Preheat the oven to 200°C (400°F), Gas Mark 6.

Put the cauliflower florets and inner leaves into a roasting tray. Drizzle over the olive oil, sprinkle with the turmeric and season with salt and pepper, then toss to mix. Roast for 30–40 minutes until tender and nicely browned, tossing the cauliflower halfway through.

Meanwhile, for the dukkah, heat a large frying pan over a medium heat and toast all the seeds for about 5 minutes, or until they start releasing their aromas and gain a little colour. Remove from the heat and let them cool for a few minutes, then gently crush using a pestle and mortar. Stir in the chilli flakes, salt and pepper.

Once the cauliflower is ready, remove from the oven, scatter over the dukkah, or however much you like, and then the pomegranate seeds and parsley leaves and serve.

Given the season, it would be rude not to add a traditional tipple to the cranberry sauce, but this is still delicious if you prefer or need to skip the sherry – just add a splash more water.

Spiced Sherry-laced Cranberry Sauce

SERVES 4–6

150 ml (¼ pint) sherry
500 g (1 lb) fresh or frozen cranberries
75 g (3 oz) caster sugar
3 cloves
rind of 1 orange
½ cinnamon stick
150 ml (¼ pint) water

Cook the sherry in a saucepan over a medium-high heat until reduced by half.

Add the rest of the ingredients to the pan and cook over a low heat for 10 minutes or so until the cranberries have broken down a little and become slightly jammy.

Remove from the heat, and when ready to serve, remove the orange rind and cinnamon stick and serve warm.

Alternatively, make a few days in advance and leave to cool, then pour into a sterilized jar and seal with the lid. Store in the refrigerator for up to 5 days until ready to use, or freeze for up to 2 months.

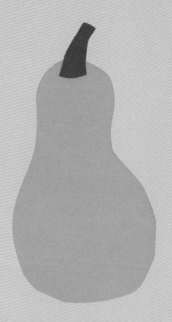

CHAPTER 4

Leftovers

A very different take on a Christmas sandwich inspired by the Mexican quesadilla, this is a wonderful way to use up nut roast (if there is any left over!), and easy to whip up if you're feeling particularly laid-back (as you should be).

Nut Roast Wraps

SERVES 2

2 ripe avocados
2 tablespoons olive oil
juice of 1 lime
1 heaped tablespoon
    chopped coriander
2 large tortilla wraps
2 heaped tablespoons
    hummus
2–3 thick slices of leftover
    nut roast (see pages 49–50
    and 51)
salt and pepper

Halve the avocados and remove the stones, then scoop out the flesh and roughly mash with 1 tablespoon of the olive oil, the lime juice, coriander and salt and pepper to taste in a bowl.

Lay the tortillas out flat on a work surface and spread 1 heaped tablespoon of the hummus over one half of each tortilla. Divide the nut roast between the tortillas, crumbling it evenly over the hummus, and lastly spoon over an equal quantity of the avocado mixture. Fold the plain half of each tortilla over the filling to make a semicircle.

Heat the remaining tablespoon of olive oil in a large frying pan over a medium heat. Place the tortillas in the pan side by side and press gently on the tops with a spatula. Cook for about 2 minutes until golden and toasted on the underside, then flip and cook for another 2 minutes until toasted on the other side.

Lift the tortillas out of the pan with the spatula, cut each in half into triangles and serve while still hot.

This is the all-time classic leftover dish that never fails to please, and a great way to use up Christmas lunch leftovers – or any cooked potato and veg you have spare. Serve with salad if you like.

Bubble & Squeak

SERVES 2

2 tablespoons olive oil
½ onion, finely diced
2 garlic cloves, very finely chopped
200 g (7 oz) leftover cooked Brussels sprouts, parsnips, carrots, cabbage or any other cooked vegetables, roughly chopped
300 g (10 oz) leftover cold mashed potatoes
handful of chopped flat leaf parsley
salt and pepper
lemon wedges, to serve

Heat the olive oil in a large frying pan and sauté the onion with the garlic over a medium heat for about 6 minutes until soft and translucent.

Add the vegetables and mashed potatoes to the pan and stir until well combined, then season to taste with salt and pepper. Cook for 2 minutes to heat through, then gently mash together until the mixture becomes one large patty. Let it cook over a medium heat for about 2 minutes until browned on the underside, then carefully flip over (hopefully the patty will stay intact, but don't worry if it doesn't!) and cook for another 2 minutes until browned on the other side.

Scatter over the parsley, cut into wedges and serve with lemon wedges on the side.

This recipe features a batter made with chickpea (gram) flour like in the Italian dish farinata. It makes a great vehicle for any leftover cooked veg you may have, not just carrots or Brussels sprouts. It's also really good for a lunchbox treat.

Carrot & Sprout Chickpea Pan Cake

SERVES 2

150 g (5 oz) gram (besan/
    chickpea) flour
½ teaspoon baking powder
½ teaspoon salt
350 ml (12 fl oz) warm water
4 tablespoons olive oil
1 red onion, cut into
    thin wedges
2 garlic cloves, very finely
    chopped
1 tablespoon roughly
    chopped rosemary leaves
65 g (2½ oz) leftover cooked
    carrots, roughly chopped
    if large pieces
65 g (2½ oz) leftover cooked
    Brussels sprouts, sliced

Whisk together the flour, baking powder and salt in a bowl. Make a well in the centre, pour in the measured warm water and 2 tablespoons of the olive oil and gradually whisk into the dry ingredients until all incorporated and you have a smooth batter. Cover with a clean tea towel and let the batter rest for 30 minutes.

Preheat the oven to 200°C (400°F), Gas Mark 6.

Heat the remaining 2 tablespoons olive oil in a large ovenproof frying pan and sauté the red onion over a medium heat for 6 minutes until softened. Add the garlic and rosemary and cook for another 2 minutes. Stir in the carrots and sprouts until well combined.

Pour over the chickpea batter and bake for 20 minutes, or until the pancake is crispy on top and cooked through. Remove from the oven, cut into wedges and serve.

These mini pies are great for a lunchtime snack with salad,
or pack up to take on a walk over the festive season.

Roasted Veg & Stuffing Hand Pies

MAKES 8

1 tablespoon olive oil
1 onion, finely chopped
1 garlic clove, very finely
  chopped
300 g (10 oz) leftover mixed
  roasted vegetables,
  roughly chopped into
  small cubes
200 g (7 oz) leftover
  Mushroom & Chestnut
  Stuffing (see page 81)
  or other vegan stuffing,
  crumbled
1 teaspoon plain flour, plus
  extra for dusting
200 ml (7 fl oz) leftover
  Mushroom & Onion
  Gravy (see page 79) or
  other vegan gravy
handful of flat leaf parsley
  leaves, chopped
500 g (1 lb) vegan puff pastry
50 ml (2 fl oz) oat milk
chilli flakes, for sprinkling
  (optional)
salt and pepper

Heat the olive oil in a large frying pan and sauté the onion with garlic over a medium heat for about 6 minutes until softened. Stir in the vegetables and stuffing and cook for a minute. Then stir in the flour, pour over the gravy and cook, stirring constantly, for 2 minutes until the sauce thickens and the vegetables are well coated, adding a splash of water if the mixture is too thick. Season to taste with salt and pepper and stir in the parsley. Remove from the heat and let the mixture cool completely.

Preheat the oven to 200°C (400°F), Gas Mark 6. Line 2 baking trays with nonstick baking paper.

Roll out the pastry on a lightly floured work surface until about 2.5 mm (⅛ inch) thick. Using an upturned saucer or bowl as a guide, cut out 8 circles 14 cm (5½ inches) in diameter. Divide the vegetable mixture into 8 equal portions. Spoon one portion on to one half of a pastry circle. Brush round the edge with oat milk, fold the plain half over the filling to make a semicircle and press the edges together to seal. Then either crimp the edges by pressing with a fork or pinching with your fingers. Repeat with the remaining pastry circles and filling.

Place the pies on the lined trays, brush all over with the remaining oat milk and sprinkle with chilli flakes, if you like, then make a little hole in each for the steam to escape. Bake for 20–25 minutes until golden brown and puffed up. Remove from the oven and serve hot, or once cooled.

A warming, nutritious bowl for a cold day, you can swap out the carrots and parsnips for just about any leftover roasted veg. Roasted butternut squash also works really well here.

Carrot & Parsnip Dhal

SERVES 4

2 tablespoons vegetable oil
1 tablespoon cumin seeds
1 onion, finely chopped
2.5 cm (1 inch) piece of
  fresh root ginger, peeled
  and grated
2 teaspoons garam masala
1 teaspoon ground coriander
200 g (7 oz) split red lentils,
  well rinsed and drained
750 ml (1¼ pints) water
1 teaspoon ground turmeric
1 tablespoon salt
300 g (10 oz) leftover roasted
  carrots, roughly chopped
300 g (10 oz) leftover roasted
  parsnips, roughly chopped
2 large handfuls of spinach
  leaves, roughly chopped
handful of coriander leaves,
  to serve

Heat the vegetable oil in a large saucepan, add the cumin seeds and let them sizzle over a medium heat for a few seconds. Add the onion and cook for about 8 minutes until soft and translucent.

Stir in the ginger, garam masala and ground coriander and cook for another 2 minutes. Add the lentils and stir well to combine, then pour in the measured water, bring to a simmer and cook gently for 20 minutes.

Skim any residue from the surface of the mixture, then stir in the turmeric, salt and roasted vegetables and cook for another 15 minutes, or until the lentils are tender and can be mashed slightly with the back of the spoon.

Stir the spinach through the dhal and cook for another 2 minutes, or just until wilted. Serve in bowls, topped with the coriander leaves.

Vibrant and sweet from the red cabbage and sour from the sauerkraut, this simple soup is very refreshing and soothing after a day of heavy feasting.

Red Cabbage & Sauerkraut Soup

SERVES 4–6

2 tablespoons olive oil, plus extra for drizzling

1 large onion, finely diced

2 celery sticks, finely diced

2 carrots, peeled and finely diced

3 garlic cloves, very finely chopped

300 g (10 oz) leftover cooked red cabbage

300 g (10 oz) sauerkraut

leaves from 2 thyme sprigs

1 litre (1¾ pints) hot vegan vegetable stock

2 tomatoes, chopped

salt and pepper

handful of dill fronds, roughly chopped, to garnish

Heat the olive oil in a large saucepan and sauté the onion, celery and carrots with the garlic over a medium heat for about 8 minutes until softened.

Stir in the red cabbage, sauerkraut and thyme leaves, then pour over the hot stock. Season to taste with salt and pepper and simmer for 20 minutes to allow the flavours to meld.

Just before serving, stir in the tomatoes. Ladle into bowls and top with a drizzle of olive oil, a twist of freshly ground black pepper and the chopped dill.

It always feels so virtuous to have a pile of greens for a meal, especially after indulging at Christmas. But you can make them taste amazing by topping them with crispy-fried chilli-flavoured tofu, served on a bed of steaming rice.

Greens Stir-fry with Crispy Chilli Tofu

SERVES 2

125 g (4 oz) jasmine or
  sushi rice
4 tablespoons sesame oil
300 g (10 oz) firm tofu,
  wrapped in kitchen paper
  and squeezed of any excess
  moisture, then cut into
  1 cm (½ inch) cubes
2 tablespoons vegan crispy
  chilli oil
500 g (1 lb) cooked leftover
  greens, such as kale,
  Brussels sprouts or
  broccoli, sliced if large
  pieces
4 garlic cloves, thinly sliced
2 tablespoons light soy sauce,
  plus extra (optional) for
  drizzling
2 tablespoons Shaoxing
  rice wine

First, start cooking the rice according to the packet instructions.

While the rice is cooking, heat the sesame oil in a large wok or frying pan and fry the tofu over a high heat, tossing every now and then, for about 2 minutes until crispy sides on all sides. Remove with a slotted spoon, reserving the oil in the pan, and drain on a plate lined with kitchen paper. Then transfer to a bowl and toss with the crispy chilli oil.

Stir-fry the greens with the garlic slices in the same pan over a high heat for about 2 minutes until they are nicely charred. Add the soy sauce and rice wine and cook for another minute.

Once the rice is cooked, divide it between 2 bowls, top with the stir-fried greens and then add a good heap of the crispy chilli tofu. Drizzle with a little more soy sauce if you want it salty and saucier.

This is a delicious way to get as many veg into a meal as possible. The mashed potato topping is lightened with broccoli, which also makes it a fun colour.

Broccoli Mash 'Shepherd's' Pie SERVES 4–6

1 tablespoon olive oil
1 onion, finely diced
2 celery sticks, finely diced
4 garlic cloves, very finely
    chopped
400 g (13 oz) mixed leftover
    roasted vegetables, such
    as squash, parsnips and
    Brussels sprouts, roughly
    chopped
1 tablespoon plain flour
400 g (13 oz) can chickpeas,
    drained and rinsed
leaves from 2 thyme sprigs
10 sun-dried tomatoes,
    roughly chopped
1 tablespoon tomato purée
1 tablespoon balsamic
    vinegar
200 ml (7 fl oz) hot vegan
    vegetable stock
100 g (3½ oz) frozen peas
salt and pepper

Broccoli mash
625 g (1¼ lb) white potatoes,
    peeled and chopped
300 g (10 oz) broccoli,
    broken into florets
50 g (2 oz) vegan butter
50 ml (2 fl oz) oat milk

For the broccoli mash, cook the potatoes in a large saucepan of salted boiling water for about 8 minutes, then add the broccoli and cook for another 2–3 minutes until you can push a fork into both the potato and broccoli easily.

Drain the vegetables and let them steam dry for a few minutes, then return to the pan and mash well with the vegan butter, gradually adding the oat milk, as you may not need it all. Season to taste with salt and pepper and set aside.

Heat the olive oil in a large frying pan and sauté the onion and celery with the garlic over a medium heat for about 6 minutes until softened. Stir in the roast vegetables and cook for another minute or so.

Meanwhile, preheat the oven to 200°C (400°F), Gas Mark 6.

Stir in the flour until well combined, then add the chickpeas, thyme leaves, sun-dried tomatoes, tomato purée and balsamic vinegar. Pour over the hot stock, stir thoroughly and then simmer for about 8–10 minutes, or until the mixture thickens.

Mix in the peas and season to taste with salt and pepper, then transfer the mixture to a deep medium-sized ovenproof dish. Spoon over the broccoli mash, rough up the surface with a fork so that it will get extra crispy and bake for 30–40 minutes until the topping is golden brown. Remove from the oven and serve.

Quick and easy, and full of fragrant flavour, this curry recipe also works perfectly with any leftover roasted roots, such as sweet potato, carrots, parsnips, celeriac or potatoes, or a mixture of any of them.

Roast Butternut Squash Curry   SERVES 4

2 tablespoons vegetable oil

1 large onion, finely diced

4 garlic cloves, grated

2.5 cm (1 inch) piece of fresh root ginger, peeled and grated

1 teaspoon cumin seeds

1 tablespoon garam masala

1 teaspoon ground turmeric

1 teaspoon ground coriander

½ teaspoon chilli powder

2 tablespoons tomato purée

2 tablespoons nut butter, such as almond or peanut

500 g (1 lb) leftover roasted butternut squash, roughly chopped

1 teaspoon salt

400 ml (14 fl oz) can coconut milk

100 g (3½ oz) spinach leaves

Heat the vegetable oil in a large saucepan or deep frying pan and sauté the onion over a medium heat for 6 minutes until softened. Then add the garlic and ginger and cook for 2 minutes.

Stir in the cumin seeds and fry for a minute. Then stir through the rest of the spices and cook for 1–2 minutes to flavour the onion. Add the tomato purée and then the nut butter, breaking it up with your spoon to disperse it.

Add the roasted squash and salt, then pour over the coconut milk and stir well. Cook for 10 minutes until the curry thickens.

Just before serving, stir the spinach through the curry and cook for another 2 minutes, or just until wilted. Serve with rice or roti, if preferred.

The recipe obviously depends on you having any roast potatoes left over, which may be a rare occurrence, given their universal popularity. But this salad is so delicious that you may decide to cook up extra roast potatoes just to make it!

Roast Potato Salad with Pickled Onions

SERVES 4

2 tablespoons olive oil
1 tablespoon lemon juice
2 garlic cloves, crushed
500 g (1 lb) roast potatoes
200 g (7 oz) salad leaves, such
   as rocket or watercress
1 tablespoon capers
handful of flat leaf parsley
   leaves, chopped
½ teaspoon sumac
salt and pepper

Pickled onions
1 red onion, finely sliced
100 ml (3½ fl oz) vegan
   white wine vinegar
1 tablespoon caster sugar
1 teaspoon salt

First make the pickled onions. Mix together all the ingredients in a non-reactive bowl, then set aside for at least 20 minutes.

To make the dressing for the roast potatoes, whisk together the olive oil, lemon juice, garlic and a pinch of salt and pepper in a large bowl.

If you want to crisp up the roast potatoes again, you can either reheat them in the oven or cook them in a frying pan in a little olive oil, or just use them cold straight from the refrigerator.

Add the roast potatoes to the dressing along with the salad leaves, capers and parsley and toss to combine.

Serve scattered with the pickled onions and sprinkled with the sumac.

*If you have leftover mincemeat from the Mincemeat & Apple
Strudel (see page 155) or just a jar hanging around, this is a nice
way to jazz up pancakes – a perfect Christmas Day breakfast treat.
They can be served with maple syrup or a squeeze of lemon juice
and a sprinkling of sugar, or try them with vegan soured cream.*

Mincemeat Pancakes

SERVES 4–6

400 ml (14 fl oz) oat or
almond milk

1½ tablespoons apple cider
vinegar

1 tablespoon vanilla extract

300 g (10 oz) plain flour

2 teaspoons baking powder

pinch of salt

2 tablespoons golden caster
sugar

finely grated zest of 1 orange

8 heaped tablespoons vegan
mincemeat

vegetable or coconut oil,
for frying

Whisk together the oat or almond milk, vinegar and vanilla
extract in a jug.

Whisk together the flour, baking powder, salt, sugar and
orange zest in a large bowl. Make a well in the centre, pour in
the oat or almond milk mixture and gradually whisk into the
dry ingredients until all incorporated and you have a smooth
batter. Fold in the mincemeat, then cover with a clean tea
towel and let the batter rest for 30 minutes.

Once the batter has rested, heat a little drizzle of oil in a
large nonstick frying pan, ladle the batter into the pan,
enough to make the size of pancake you prefer, and cook
until bubbles form on the surface. Then flip over and
cook until golden brown on both sides. Remove and keep
warm on an ovenproof plate in a low oven while you repeat
with the remaining batter, stacking the cooked pancakes on
the plate. Once all the batter is cooked, serve the pancakes
with whatever accompaniments you like.

These spiced, fruity muffins are great for breakfast or with a cup of tea later in the day. Using the homemade sherry-flavoured cranberry sauce turns them into an extra-special treat, but the jarred stuff also works well and is kid-friendly.

Cranberry Sauce Muffins

MAKES 12

275 g (9 oz) plain flour

2 teaspoons baking powder

½ teaspoon bicarbonate
   of soda

½ teaspoon salt

1 teaspoon ground
   cinnamon

175 g (6 oz) caster sugar

finely grated zest of ½ orange

75 g (3 oz) vegan butter,
   melted

1 tablespoon flaxseed,
   soaked in 3 tablespoons
   water for 10 minutes
   to activate

100 g (3½ oz) vegan yogurt

2 teaspoons vanilla extract

200 g (7 oz) leftover Spiced
   Sherry-laced Cranberry
   Sauce (see page 86) or
   shop-bought cranberry
   sauce

Preheat the oven to 190°C (375°F), Gas Mark 5. Line a 12-cup muffin tray with paper muffin cases.

Whisk together the flour, baking powder, bicarbonate of soda, salt, cinnamon, sugar and orange zest in a large bowl. Make a well in the centre, pour in the melted vegan butter, activated flaxseed solution, vegan yogurt and vanilla extract and fold gently together until just combined. Then fold in 150 g (5 oz) of the cranberry sauce until just swirled through the batter.

Scoop the muffin batter evenly into the muffin cases, top each muffin with a last spoonful of cranberry sauce and bake for 25–30 minutes, or until the muffins have risen and are springy to the touch. Remove from the oven and leave to cool for 5 minutes in the tray, then transfer to a wire rack to cool further.

CHAPTER 5

Baking

This festive-shaped sharing bread makes an ideal centrepiece for your Christmas party table and provides a fun communal eating experience. The swirl of pesto gives it a punchy savoury flavour.

Pesto Tear 'n' Share Christmas Tree

SERVES 4–6

500 ml (17 fl oz) lukewarm water
10 g (⅓ oz) fast-action dried yeast
750 g (1½ lb) strong white flour, plus extra dusting
10 g (⅓ oz) fine salt
1 tablespoon sugar
75 g (3 oz) vegan butter, softened
vegetable oil, for greasing
150 g (5 oz) shop-bought vegan pesto
handful of roughly chopped flat leaf parsley leaves

Mix together the measured lukewarm water and yeast in a jug and set aside for about 8 minutes until the mixture is frothy and the yeast is activated.

Meanwhile, beat together the flour, salt, sugar and 50 g (2 oz) of the vegan butter in a stand mixer or in a large bowl with a wooden spoon until well combined.

Once the yeast mixture is ready, stir it into the flour mixture. If using a mixer, knead with the dough hook on a medium speed for 5 minutes. If making by hand, knead on a lightly floured work surface for 8 minutes, or until the dough is smooth, soft and springy to the touch. Grease the mixing bowl, then return the dough, cover the bowl with a clean tea towel and let it rise in a warm, dry place for an hour, or until doubled in size.

After the dough has risen, knead the dough roughly in the bowl for a few minutes to knock the excess air out of it until it deflates, then scrape out on to a lightly floured work surface. Roll out into a large rectangle, roughly 40 × 55 cm (16 × 22 inches) – the dough should be about 2.5 mm (⅛ inch) thick.

recipe continues overleaf

Line a large baking tray with nonstick baking paper. Spread the vegan pesto evenly over the surface of the dough, then start tightly rolling up from one longer side to the opposite longer side until you have a long log shape. Slice the log into 5 cm (2 inch) thick rounds, then tuck the loose end of each round underneath the swirl so that the vegan pesto is contained within the swirl. Arrange the rounds flat on the lined tray in the shape of a Christmas tree. Cover with the clean tea towel and let the dough rise for another 30 minutes.

When the dough is almost ready, preheat the oven to 200°C (400°F), Gas Mark 6.

Dot little pieces of the remaining vegan butter over the swirls, then bake for 30–40 minutes, or until well risen and golden brown. Serve immediately scattered with chopped parsley leaves.

*Crisp and aromatic, these crackers are delicious on their own as a
nibble, or great to serve with any savoury vegan spreads or dips, such
as the Lemony Artichoke Pâté (see page 15). They will keep for up to a
week in an airtight container, so a really handy prep-ahead item.*

Seedy Rosemary Crackers

MAKES 30–40

275 g (9 oz) plain flour,
    plus extra for dusting
1½ teaspoons sea salt flakes,
    plus extra for topping
1 teaspoon sugar
½ teaspoon cracked
    black pepper
30 g (1 oz) sesame seeds,
    plus extra for topping
30 g (1 oz) nigella seeds,
    plus extra for topping
20 g (¾ oz) fennel seeds,
    plus extra for topping
1 tablespoon finely chopped
    rosemary leaves
65 ml (2½ fl oz) olive oil
125 ml (4 fl oz) warm water
2 teaspoons chilli flakes, for
    topping (optional)

Preheat the oven to 220°C (425°F), Gas Mark 7. Line
2 baking trays with nonstick baking paper.

Mix together all the ingredients, except the chilli flakes
(if using), in a large bowl and bring the mixture together
with your hands into a dough. Knead in the bowl until
soft and elastic.

Cut the dough in half and leave one half in the bowl,
covered with a clean tea towel. Roll out the other half on a
lightly floured work surface into a rectangle about 2.5 mm
(⅛ inch) thick.

Scatter over the extra seeds and sea salt, along with the chilli
flakes if using, ensuring they are evenly distributed, and
gently press into the surface of the dough with a rolling
pin. Roughly cut into squares, using a ruler for guidance if
preferred, gathering together and rerolling the trimmings
to cut out more, then prick all over with a fork. Repeat this
process with the remaining half of the dough.

Place the crackers on the lined trays, spaced slightly apart,
and bake for 10–12 minutes, or until crisp and golden.
Remove from the oven, then transfer the crackers to a wire
rack to cool completely.

These hearty, feisty muffins make a delicious savoury breakfast, and are great for a lunchtime snack too. If you are feeling extra decadent, enjoy them warm from the oven with extra vegan butter slathered on top.

Spicy Cornbread Muffins

MAKES 12

1 tablespoon olive oil

1 red onion, finely diced

1 red pepper, cored, deseeded and cut into small chunks

1 yellow pepper, cored, deseeded and cut into small chunks

150 g (5 oz) cornmeal or fine quick-cook polenta

150 g (5 oz) plain flour

1 tablespoon caster sugar

1 teaspoon baking powder

1 teaspoon bicarbonate of soda

½ teaspoon salt

½ teaspoon black pepper

225 ml (7½ fl oz) oat milk

1 tablespoon apple cider vinegar

150 g (5 oz) vegan butter, melted

100 g (3½ oz) canned sweetcorn, drained

100 g (3½ oz) sliced jalapeños from a jar, drained, 12 slices reserved for topping, the remainder roughly chopped

Preheat the oven to 200°C (400°F), Gas Mark 6. Line a 12-cup muffin tray with paper muffin cases.

Heat the olive oil in a large frying pan and sauté the onion over a medium heat for about 6 minutes until softened. Then stir in the peppers and fry for 8 minutes. Remove from the heat and let the mixture cool.

Whisk together the cornmeal, flour, sugar, baking powder, bicarbonate of soda, salt and pepper in a large bowl. In a separate bowl, whisk together the oat milk, vinegar and melted vegan butter. Make a well in the dry ingredients, pour in the wet ingredients and fold gently together until just combined. Then fold in the onion and pepper mixture, sweetcorn and chopped jalapeños.

Scoop the muffin batter evenly into the muffin cases – you want them fairly full – then top each one with a jalapeño slice. Bake for 20–25 minutes, or until they are firm to the touch. Remove from the oven and let the muffins cool in the tray for 5 minutes, then transfer to a wire rack to cool further or serve warm.

This is the perfect way to use up any pastry scraps you may have left over from other recipes and turn them into something delicious. Simply keep all your pastry scraps together – it can be a mixture of shortcrust and puff pastry – wrapped closely in the refrigerator, which you can add to over the course of at least a few days.

Pastry Scrap Sun-dried Tomato Pinwheels

MAKES 36–40

300 g (10 oz) vegan pastry scraps (see intro)
plain flour, for dusting
4 tablespoons sun-dried tomato paste
½ teaspoon dried parsley
pinch of pepper

Preheat the oven to 190°C (375°F), Gas Mark 5. Line a baking tray with nonstick baking paper.

Gather together the pastry scraps and knead slightly to form a smooth ball. Roll out on a lightly floured work surface into a rectangle about 2.5 mm (⅛ inch) thick.

Spread over the sun-dried tomato paste and sprinkle over the parsley and pepper.

Roll up the pastry tightly from one longer side to the opposite longer side until you have a long sausage shape. Using a sharp knife, slice into 1 cm (½ inch) thick rounds and place flat on the lined tray, spaced slightly apart.

Bake for 8–10 minutes, or until slightly puffed up and golden brown.

These scones are flavourful enough to enjoy on their own, or try them slathered in Christmas chutney or served with a soup. They make a welcome treat in the lull between Christmas and New Year. You can also freeze the scones before baking and just bake from frozen, for an extra 5 minutes, whenever you fancy a savoury snack.

Savoury Scones

MAKES 12

500 g (1 lb) plain flour,
  plus extra for dusting
150 g (5 oz) vegan butter,
  chilled and cubed
1½ tablespoons baking
  powder
1 teaspoon salt
2 tablespoons
  nutritional yeast
1 teaspoon sweet
  smoked paprika
½ teaspoon pepper
½ teaspoon chilli flakes
10 g (⅓ oz) chives,
  finely chopped
200 ml (7 fl oz) oat milk,
  plus extra for brushing

Put the flour into a bowl a large bowl, add the vegan butter and rub in with your fingertips until the mixture resembles coarse breadcrumbs. Stir in the baking powder, salt, nutritional yeast, paprika, pepper, chilli flakes and chives until well combined. Gradually mix in the oat milk and bring the mixture together with your hands into a dough.

Turn the dough out on to a lightly floured work surface and pat into a square. Fold the square over in half, turn once to the left and pat it back into a square. Then repeat the folding and turning process once more. This will create nice flaky layers in the scones. Let the dough rest for about 15 minutes.

Preheat the oven to 200°C (400°F), Gas Mark 6. Line a baking tray with nonstick baking paper.

Roll out the dough until about 2.5 cm (1 inch) thick, dusting with a little more flour if it is sticky. Roll or pat the dough into a 23 × 15 cm (9 × 6 inches) rectangle and cut in half lengthways and into thirds widthways to make 6 squares, then cut each square diagonally into triangles.

Place the scones on the lined tray, spaced apart, brush with oat milk and bake for 20 minutes, or until well risen and golden brown. Remove from the oven, then transfer to a wire rack to cool. Serve warm.

A classic made vegan, you can bake the cake up to 2 weeks in advance and store undecorated and well wrapped in an airtight container for up to 1 week, during which time you can feed it with extra rum or brandy every now and then, depending on how boozy you want it, up until at least a couple of days before icing so that the surface is dry. It's best to decorate it the day before serving so that the icing is thoroughly set.

Christmas Cake

SERVES 10–12

250 g (8 oz) **vegan butter**
   or coconut oil, plus extra
   for greasing
175 g (6 oz) **soft light brown**
   sugar
finely grated **zest of 2 oranges**
   and juice of 1
finely grated **zest and juice**
   of 1 lemon (reserve 1
   tablespoon juice for the
   icing – see page 126)
150 ml (¼ pint) **rum or**
   brandy, plus extra
   (optional) for feeding
875 g (1¾ lb) **mixed dried**
   fruit of your choice,
   such as sultanas, raisins,
   currants, cranberries and
   chopped figs and apricots
100 g (3½ oz) **chopped**
   candied peel
175 g (6 oz) **plain flour**
125 g (4 oz) **ground almonds**
1 teaspoon **baking powder**
¼ teaspoon **salt**

Preheat the oven to 160°C (325°F), Gas Mark 3. Grease a deep 20 cm (8 inch) round cake tin and line with nonstick baking paper.

Melt the vegan butter or coconut oil in a saucepan along with the brown sugar, citrus zest and juice and rum or brandy (if using). Bring to the boil and simmer for 2 minutes, then remove from the heat.

Add the dried fruit and candied peel to a large bowl, pour over the vegan butter/coconut oil mixture and stir well.

In a separate bowl, whisk together the flour, ground almonds, baking powder, salt and spices.

Mix the apple purée into the dried fruit mixture, then fold in the flour mixture until just combined.

Pour the cake batter into the lined tin, smooth the surface with a spatula and bake for 1½ hours. Remove the cake from the oven and let it cool completely in the tin. Once cooled, pierce holes all over the top of the cake with a skewer, drizzle over 2 tablespoons rum or brandy and let it soak in. Make sure the surface is fully dry before decorating.

recipe continues overleaf

Meanwhile, make the glaze. In a separate bowl, gently whisk the almond milk and maple syrup together until combined. Brush the pastry border with a little of the glaze, then lay over the larger circle of pastry and press the edges together to seal. Then either crimp by pressing with a fork or pinching with your fingers.

Using a knife, lightly score a pattern in the top of the pastry, then brush all over with the remaining glaze. Chill in the refrigerator for 30 minutes–1 hour.

When ready to bake, preheat the oven to 190°C (375°F), Gas Mark 5.

Bake the cake for 35–40 minutes, or until the pastry is golden brown. Remove from the oven and let it cool for 30 minutes or so, then cut into slices and serve.

It is traditional in many countries to celebrate Twelfth Night or Epiphany with a king or kings cake, and this recipe is based on France's version, galette des rois, *with a trinket or* fève *hidden within – in this case an almond – the finder of which is made king or queen for the day. If you're feeling extra creative, you can make a little crown out of cardboard to decorate the centre of the cake and then to crown your king or queen!*

King Cake

SERVES 6–8

150 g (5 oz) vegan butter, softened
175 g (6 oz) caster sugar
50 g (2 oz) plain flour, plus extra for dusting
½ teaspoon baking powder
200 g (7 oz) ground almonds
finely grated zest of 1 orange
125 ml (4 fl oz) almond milk,
1 tablespoon almond extract
500 g (1 lb) vegan puff pastry
1 whole almond

Glaze
2 tablespoons almond milk
1 tablespoon maple syrup

Beat together the vegan butter and sugar in a stand mixer or in a large bowl with an electric hand whisk or a wooden spoon until pale and fluffy.

In a separate bowl, whisk together the flour, baking powder, ground almonds and orange zest. Fold half the mixture into the vegan butter mixture, then pour in half the 125 ml (4 fl oz) almond milk with the almond extract and mix until combined. Repeat with the remaining flour mixture and almond milk.

Line a large baking tray with nonstick baking paper. Cut the pastry into 2 pieces, one slightly larger than the other. Roll out the smaller piece of pastry on a lightly floured work surface into a circle about 20 cm (8 inches) in diameter (you can cut around a cake tin or pie dish to make a perfect circle if you like). Roll out the other piece of pastry into a larger circle, about 25 cm (10 inches) in diameter.

Place the smaller circle on the lined tray and spread over the filling mixture, leaving a 1.5 cm (¾ inch) clear border around the edge, then bury the whole almond in the filling.

recipe continues overleaf

Meanwhile, make the glaze. In a separate bowl, gently whisk the almond milk and maple syrup together until combined. Brush the pastry border with a little of the glaze, then lay over the larger circle of pastry and press the edges together to seal. Then either crimp by pressing with a fork or pinching with your fingers.

Using a knife, lightly score a pattern in the top of the pastry, then brush all over with the remaining glaze. Chill in the refrigerator for 30 minutes–1 hour.

When ready to bake, preheat the oven to 190°C (375°F), Gas Mark 5.

Bake the cake for 35–40 minutes, or until the pastry is golden brown. Remove from the oven and let it cool for 30 minutes or so, then cut into slices and serve.

A classic made vegan, you can bake the cake up to 2 weeks in advance and store undecorated and well wrapped in an airtight container for up to 1 week, during which time you can feed it with extra rum or brandy every now and then, depending on how boozy you want it, up until at least a couple of days before icing so that the surface is dry. It's best to decorate it the day before serving so that the icing is thoroughly set.

Christmas Cake

SERVES 10–12

250 g (8 oz) vegan butter
   or coconut oil, plus extra
   for greasing
175 g (6 oz) soft light brown
   sugar
finely grated zest of 2 oranges
   and juice of 1
finely grated zest and juice
   of 1 lemon (reserve 1
   tablespoon juice for the
   icing – see page 126)
150 ml (¼ pint) rum or
   brandy, plus extra
   (optional) for feeding
875 g (1¾ lb) mixed dried
   fruit of your choice,
   such as sultanas, raisins,
   currants, cranberries and
   chopped figs and apricots
100 g (3½ oz) chopped
   candied peel
175 g (6 oz) plain flour
125 g (4 oz) ground almonds
1 teaspoon baking powder
¼ teaspoon salt

Preheat the oven to 160°C (325°F), Gas Mark 3. Grease a deep 20 cm (8 inch) round cake tin and line with nonstick baking paper.

Melt the vegan butter or coconut oil in a saucepan along with the brown sugar, citrus zest and juice and rum or brandy (if using). Bring to the boil and simmer for 2 minutes, then remove from the heat.

Add the dried fruit and candied peel to a large bowl, pour over the vegan butter/coconut oil mixture and stir well.

In a separate bowl, whisk together the flour, ground almonds, baking powder, salt and spices.

Mix the apple purée into the dried fruit mixture, then fold in the flour mixture until just combined.

Pour the cake batter into the lined tin, smooth the surface with a spatula and bake for 1½ hours. Remove the cake from the oven and let it cool completely in the tin. Once cooled, pierce holes all over the top of the cake with a skewer, drizzle over 2 tablespoons rum or brandy and let it soak in. Make sure the surface is fully dry before decorating.

recipe continues overleaf

2 teaspoons ground
   cinnamon
¾ teaspoon ground ginger
½ teaspoon ground mace
¼ teaspoon ground cloves
¼ teaspoon ground nutmeg
225 g (7½ oz) apple purée

Icing
625 g (1¼ lb) icing sugar,
   plus extra for dusting
75 ml (3 fl oz) aquafaba
1 tablespoon lemon juice
4 tablespoons apricot jam
500 g (1 lb) vegan marzipan

When you are ready to decorate, whisk together the icing sugar, aquafaba and lemon juice in a large bowl until you have a stiff and glossy icing. Cover the bowl with clingfilm until needed.

Heat the apricot jam in a small saucepan, then brush over the top and sides of the cake. On a work surface lightly dusted with icing sugar, roll out the marzipan into a rough circle until about 2.5 mm (⅛ inch) thick. Lay carefully over the cake and gently smooth it on to the top and down around the sides so that there is no air trapped inside. Neaten by smoothing over with the flat of your palm or the rolling pin and trim away any excess.

Using a spatula or the back of a spoon, spread over the icing in swoops and flicks to look like snow, or you can make it completely smooth. Let the icing set completely for at least a few hours before cutting.

A lovely moist cake with lots of warming spice encased in a fluffy frosting, this is just so good served in generous slices with a huge mug of tea or coffee.

Spiced Pumpkin Cake

SERVES 8

400 g (13 oz) pumpkin purée
250 ml (8 fl oz) vegetable oil,
  plus extra for greasing
250 g (8 oz) soft light
  brown sugar
2 tablespoons flaxseed,
  soaked in 6 tablespoons
  water for 10 minutes
  to activate
1 teaspoon vanilla extract
250 g (8 oz) plain flour
2½ teaspoons baking powder
1 teaspoon bicarbonate
  of soda
1 teaspoon salt
2 teaspoons ground
  cinnamon
½ teaspoon ground nutmeg
½ teaspoon ground ginger
¼ teaspoon ground cloves

Frosting
250 g (8 oz) vegan cream
  cheese
125 g (4 oz) vegan butter,
  softened
500 g (1 lb) icing sugar
1 teaspoon vanilla extract

Preheat the oven to 180°C (350°F), Gas Mark 4. Grease a 20 cm (8 inch) round cake tin and line with nonstick baking paper.

Whisk together the purée, vegetable oil, brown sugar, activated flaxseed and vanilla extract in a large bowl.

In a separate bowl, whisk together all the dry ingredients, then fold into the pumpkin mixture until just combined – do not overmix.

Pour the batter into the lined tin and bake for 45 minutes–1 hour until the cake is springy to the touch. Remove from the oven and let the cake cool in the tin for a few minutes, then turn out on to a wire rack to cool completely before making the frosting.

Beat together the vegan cream cheese and vegan butter in a large bowl until fluffy. Then gradually beat in the icing sugar and vanilla extract until smooth.

Cut the cake horizontally in half to make 2 layers, then sandwich the layers together with some of the frosting and spread the rest over the top and sides of the cake. Cut into slices and serve.

Crumbly buttery shortbread is always a favourite festive treat, but the addition of chocolate chips and orange zest makes these extra indulgent. Alternatively, can also use chocolate chips, if preferred. Once cooled, the shortbread can be stored for up to a week in an airtight container. Suitably packaged, they are perfect for an edible Christmas gift.

Orange Chocolate Chip Shortbread

MAKES 30–40

250 g (8 oz) vegan butter, softened

125 g (4 oz) caster sugar, plus extra for sprinkling

1 teaspoon vanilla extract

350 g (11½ oz) plain flour, plus extra for dusting

finely grated zest of 2 oranges

110 g (3¾ oz) vegan dark or dairy-free milk chocolate, chopped into small chunks

Beat together the vegan butter and sugar in a stand mixer or in a large bowl with an electric hand whisk or a wooden spoon until pale and fluffy, then mix in the vanilla extract.

Fold in the flour, orange zest and chocolate chunks and bring the mixture together with your hands until it just forms a dough. Shape the dough into a disc, wrap in clingfilm and chill in the refrigerator for 30 minutes.

Preheat the oven to 180°C (350°F), Gas Mark 4. Line a large baking tray with nonstick baking paper.

Roll out the shortbread dough on a lightly floured work surface until 1 cm (½ inch) thick, then use cookie cutters to cut out whatever shapes you like, such as stars or Christmas trees, gathering together and rerolling the trimmings to cut out more.

Place the shortbread on the lined tray, spaced apart, and sprinkle with caster sugar. Bake for 10–12 minutes until cooked but only lightly coloured – the shortbread is best when it is a little soft. Remove from the oven, then transfer to a wire rack to cool completely before serving.

A vegan take on the traditional Mexican wedding cookie, these crumbly and nutty biscuits melt in the mouth. They look very festive as well as being irresistible to eat. Once cooled, the cookies can be stored for up to a week in an airtight container.

Snowball Cookies

MAKES 36–40

140 g (4½ oz) pecan nuts
250 g (8 oz) vegan butter, softened
100 g (3½ oz) icing sugar, plus 150 g (5 oz) for coating
2 teaspoons vanilla extract
300 g (10 oz) plain flour
¾ teaspoon salt

Preheat the oven to 180°C (350°F), Gas Mark 4.

Spread the pecans out on a baking tray and toast for about 10 minutes. Remove from the oven (turn the oven off) and let them cool.

Pulse the cooled pecans in a food processor until finely chopped – do not overprocess, otherwise the nuts will turn into butter.

Beat together the vegan butter and the 100 g (3½ oz) icing sugar in a stand mixer or in a large bowl with an electric hand whisk or a wooden spoon until pale and fluffy, then mix in the vanilla extract.

In a separate bowl, whisk together the flour, salt and finely chopped pecans. Fold into the vegan butter mixture and bring the mixture together with your hands until it just forms a dough. Shape the dough into a disc, wrap in clingfilm and chill in the refrigerator for 1 hour.

Preheat the oven to 180°C (350°F), Gas Mark 4. Line 2 baking trays with nonstick baking paper.

Form the cookie dough into walnut-sized balls and place on the lined trays, spaced slightly apart. Bake for about 12–15 minutes until lightly coloured.

Remove from the oven and let the cookies cool slightly, then roll in the remaining icing sugar until well coated. Place on a wire rack to cool completely.

You can make these gingerbread cookies as simple or as fancy as you like, or turn them into tree decorations by making a hole in the top to thread with string or ribbon (make the hole large enough to allow for the cookie to swell and close up the hole a little when baking). If you're feeling super creative, use the recipe to make a whole gingerbread house – there are some great templates to be found online.

Iced Gingerbread

MAKES 30–40

125 g (4 oz) vegan butter, softened
250 g (8 oz) golden syrup
100 g (3½ oz) molasses
425 g (14 oz) plain flour, plus extra for dusting
½ teaspoon salt
1½ teaspoons ground ginger
1 teaspoon ground cinnamon
½ teaspoon ground nutmeg
¼ teaspoon ground cloves

Icing
500 g (1 lb) icing sugar
75 ml (3 fl oz) aquafaba
1 tablespoon lemon juice

Beat together the vegan butter, golden syrup and molasses in a bowl until well combined.

In a separate bowl, whisk together the flour, salt and spices. Fold into the vegan butter mixture until just combined, then knead with your hands in the bowl until you have a smooth dough. Shape the dough into a disc, wrap in clingfilm and chill in the refrigerator for 30 minutes–1 hour.

Line 2 baking trays with nonstick baking paper. Roll out the dough on a lightly floured work surface until no more than 5 mm (¼ inch) thick. Use cookie cutters to cut out whatever shapes you like, such as gingerbread people or snowflakes, gathering together and rerolling the trimmings to cut out more. Place the gingerbread on the lined trays, spaced slightly apart and chill in the refrigerator for 20 minutes or so.

Meanwhile, preheat the oven to 180°C (350°F), Gas Mark 4.

Bake the gingerbread for about 10–12 minutes, or until they are a little firm to the touch. Remove from the oven, then transfer to a wire rack to cool while you make the icing.

recipe continues overleaf

Whisk together the icing ingredients in a bowl until you have a soft but stiff icing, adding a little water if too thick, or more icing sugar if too runny.

Pipe the icing on to the gingerbread using a disposable piping bag fitted with a small round writing nozzle, or you can just snip off the tip of the piping bag to make a small piping hole. Alternatively, simply drizzle the icing on with a spoon. Let the icing set for a couple of hours before serving.

Inspired by the classic Mexican tres leches *cake, so called because of the three types of milk it uses, this dairy-free delight is soft and fluffy and light as air, like eating a cloud. It's the perfect dessert to end a big celebratory meal, especially for those who are fans of coconut.*

Coconut Cloud Cake

SERVES 8

Sponge

250 ml (8 fl oz) coconut milk
125 ml (4 fl oz) lukewarm
    water
2 tablespoons white vinegar
1 teaspoon vanilla extract
350 g (11½ oz) plain flour
1½ teaspoons baking powder
½ teaspoon bicarbonate
    of soda
1 teaspoon salt
¼ teaspoon ground nutmeg
200 g (7 oz) caster sugar
100 g (3½ oz) coconut oil,
    melted, plus extra for
    greasing
100 ml (3½ fl oz) aquafaba

Soaking mixture

200 g (7 oz) vegan condensed
    milk
150 ml (¼ pint) coconut milk
50 ml (2 fl oz) oat or almond
    milk

For the sponge, preheat the oven to 180°C (350°F), Gas Mark 4. Grease a 23 cm (9 inch) round cake tin or ovenproof dish – preferably something you would like to serve the cake in.

Whisk together the coconut milk, measured lukewarm water, 1 tablespoon of the vinegar and the vanilla extract in a jug and let the mixture stand for a few minutes until it thickens.

In a large bowl, whisk together the flour, baking powder, bicarbonate of soda, salt, nutmeg and sugar. Whisk in the melted coconut oil and then gradually whisk in the coconut milk mixture until you have a smooth thick batter.

Whisk together the aquafaba and remaining tablespoon of vinegar in a stand mixer or in a large bowl with an electric hand whisk on a high speed for about 6–8 minutes until very thick and stiff, like meringue. Fold gently into the cake batter until just combined.

Pour the batter carefully into the greased tin or dish to avoid knocking any air out of the mixture and smooth the surface with a spatula, then bake for 30–40 minutes until springy to the touch. Remove from the oven, pierce holes all over the top of the sponge with a skewer and let it cool in the tin for 10 minutes.

recipe continues overleaf

To decorate
400 g (13 oz) coconut
    whipping cream
1 tablespoon icing sugar
pinch of salt
toasted coconut flakes
    (optional)
grated nutmeg (optional)

Whisk together the ingredients for the soaking mixture in a small bowl, then pour over the sponge and let it soak in and cool completely.

When ready to decorate, whip the coconut cream with the icing sugar and salt in a large bowl until it holds soft peaks. Spoon over the soaked sponge, scatter over some toasted coconut flakes and nutmeg, if you like, and serve the cake in generous scoops.

CHAPTER 6

Desserts

This recipe is handy for a make-ahead dessert, as you can freeze the uncooked balls of cookie dough and then bake two per person from frozen as required. The homemade praline ice cream is wonderful for sandwiching the cookies together, but any good shop-bought vegan ice cream will work well.

Chewy Ginger Cookie Ice Cream Sandwiches

MAKES ABOUT 24 COOKIES/ 12 SANDWICHES

225 g (7½ oz) vegan butter, softened
125 g (4 oz) soft dark brown sugar
100 g (3½ oz) treacle
300 g (10 oz) plain flour
1 teaspoon bicarbonate of soda
pinch of salt
1 teaspoon ground cinnamon
1 teaspoon ground ginger
¼ teaspoon ground cloves
200 g (7 oz) caster sugar
Hazelnut Praline Ice Cream (see page 147) or shop-bought vegan ice cream
50 g (2 oz) crystallized ginger, roughly chopped

Beat together the vegan butter, brown sugar and treacle in a stand mixer or in a large bowl with an electric hand whisk or a wooden spoon until pale and fluffy.

In a separate bowl, whisk together the flour, bicarbonate of soda, salt and spices. Fold into the vegan butter mixture and bring the mixture together with your hands until it just forms a dough.

Preheat the oven to 180°C (350°F), Gas Mark 4. Line 2 baking trays with nonstick baking paper.

Form the dough into walnut-sized balls, roll in the caster sugar and place on the lined trays, spaced apart. Bake for 14 minutes until still a little soft – they will firm up once they cool down. Let the cookies cool completely on the trays.

When ready to serve, sandwich the cookies together in pairs with a large scoop of vegan ice cream, then scatter the chopped crystallized ginger on to the ice cream.

When poached, quinces taste delicious, rather like honeyed pears. Pop them in a lightly spiced pudding and you have a wonderful dessert, perfect with vegan custard or vegan cream. You can use the leftover syrup for pancakes, or add a drizzle to a flute and top up with champagne. This recipe also works well with pears, though they won't need to be poached for as much time. See Wine-poached Pears with Pistachio Crumble (page 149) for guidance.

Quince Pudding

SERVES 6

Poached quinces
2 quinces, peeled and halved
125 g (4 oz) caster sugar
500 ml (17 fl oz) water
rind of 1 lemon
½ cinnamon stick
2 star anise

Pudding
75 ml (3 fl oz) almond milk
150 g (5 oz) vegan butter,
    softened, plus extra
    for greasing
150 g (5 oz) golden caster sugar
1 teaspoon vanilla extract
150 g (5 oz) plain flour
50 g (2 oz) ground almonds
½ teaspoon baking powder
pinch of salt
1 teaspoon ground cinnamon
½ teaspoon ground ginger
¼ teaspoon ground nutmeg
finely grated zest of 1 lemon

vegan custard or cream,
    to serve

For the poached quinces, mix together all the ingredients in a medium-sized saucepan. Scrunch up a sheet of nonstick baking paper and press down on top of the quinces to ensure they are submerged in the water. Bring to the boil, then reduce the heat and simmer gently for 1 hour, or until the quinces are pink and soft.

Lift out the quinces and set aside, then remove the lemon rind, cinnamon stick and star anise and cook the poaching liquid over a higher heat for 20 minutes, or until it reduces and thickens to form a syrup.

For the pudding, preheat the oven to 200°C (400°F), Gas Mark 6. Grease a 1 litre (1¾ pint) pudding basin and line the base with a circle of nonstick baking paper.

Cut the cores out of the quinces, then blend 2 quince halves with the almond milk in a blender into a smooth purée.

Beat together the vegan butter and sugar in a stand mixer or in a large bowl with an electric hand whisk or a wooden spoon until pale and fluffy. Fold in the quince purée and the vanilla extract.

recipe continues overleaf

In a separate bowl, whisk together the flour, ground almonds, baking powder, salt, spices and lemon zest. Fold into the vegan butter mixture until just combined.

Slice the remaining quince halves into thin wedges. Pour 20 g (¾ oz) of the quince syrup into the prepared pudding basin and arrange the quince wedges over the base. Spoon in the pudding batter and smooth the surface with the back of the spoon.

Place the pudding basin in a large, deep roasting tin and pour boiling water into the tin to come just over halfway up the sides of the pudding basin. Cover tightly with foil, ensuring there is enough space above the basin for the pudding to rise, and bake for 2 hours. Remove the foil and bake for another hour, or until a skewer inserted into the pudding comes out clean.

Remove from the oven, then run a knife around the edge of the pudding and carefully invert on to a large plate. Serve hot with vegan custard or vegan cream and a little extra drizzle of quince syrup.

This is a quick and easy no-churn vegan ice cream that goes really well with the both the Sticky Stem Ginger Toffee Pudding (see pages 151–2) and the Chewy Ginger Cookie Ice Cream Sandwiches (see page 143).

Hazelnut Praline Ice Cream

SERVES 8

125 g (4 oz) caster sugar
1 tablespoon water
pinch of salt
150 g (5 oz) blanched
    hazelnuts, toasted and
    roughly chopped
400 g (13 oz) vegan coconut
    whipping cream
1 vanilla pod, split
    lengthways and seeds
    scraped out
370 g (12 oz) vegan
    condensed milk

Line a baking tray with nonstick baking paper.

Heat the sugar with the measured water in a heavy-based saucepan over a gentle heat until the sugar dissolves, tilting the pan rather than stirring to ensure the sugar is caramelizing evenly. Increase the heat to medium and keep gently swirling the pan until the sugar turns a deep golden brown.

Add the salt and then the hazelnuts, and swirl the pan until they are nicely coated in the caramel. Pour the mixture carefully on to the lined tray, smoothing it out a little with a spatula so that it is not too thick in places, and let it cool and set for at least 20 minutes.

Once set, transfer the praline to a chopping board and break it up with a knife into smaller bite-sized pieces.

Whip the coconut whipping cream with the vanilla seeds in a large bowl until it holds stiff peaks. Fold in the vegan condensed milk, then pour the mixture into a freezer-safe container with a lid. Seal the container and freeze for 2 hours, giving the mixture a stir every hour, until it starts to firm up.

Remove from the freezer and fold through two-thirds of the praline until evenly distributed, then scatter the rest on top. Reseal and return to the freezer for at least another 2 hours. Remove from the freezer 20 minutes before serving.

An elegant and relatively light dessert, this makes the perfect finale to a big meal. Both the poached pears and the crumble are easy to prepare, and can be made a couple of days in advance and stored separately in the refrigerator for added convenience.

Wine-poached Pears with Pistachio Crumble

SERVES 6

Poached pears
600 ml (1 pint) vegan white wine
500 ml (17 fl oz) water
500 g (1 lb) caster sugar
1 cinnamon stick
1 vanilla pod, split lengthways and opened up slightly
peels of 2 lemons and juice of 1
6 ripe but firm pears

Pistachio crumble
200 g (7 oz) plain flour
150 g (5 oz) vegan butter, chilled and cubed
100 g (3½ oz) soft light brown sugar
60 g (2¼ oz) pistachio nuts, toasted and roughly chopped

vegan ice cream, to serve (optional)

Mix together all the ingredients for the poached pears, except the pears, in a large saucepan.

Peel the pears, keeping them whole and the stems intact, then trim their bases so that they can sit upright. Add the pears to the pan and gently stir. Using the saucepan as a guide, trace and cut a circle out of the greaseproof paper. Place on top of the liquid to keep the pears submerged.

Cook over a medium heat until the sugar starts to dissolve and the liquid begins to simmer, then reduce the heat, and cook gently for about 20 minutes, or until the pears are tender all the way through when you insert a cocktail stick but not falling apart.

Carefully lift out the pears and set aside, then remove the cinnamon stick and vanilla pod and cook the poaching liquid over a higher heat for about 20 minutes, or until it reduces and thickens to form a syrup. Set aside.

For the pistachio crumble, preheat the oven to 190°C (375°F), Gas Mark 5. Line a baking tray with nonstick baking paper.

recipe continues overleaf

Put the flour into a bowl, add the vegan butter and rub in with your fingertips until the mixture resembles coarse breadcrumbs. Stir in the brown sugar with a few splashes of water to clump some of the mixture together.

Spread the crumble out on the lined tray and bake for 30 minutes, or until crisp and golden brown. Remove from the oven and stir through the pistachios.

When ready to serve, carefully return the pears to the syrup and warm through gently. Then place a pear in each serving dish, drizzle over a little of the syrup and add a large spoonful of crumble. Serve with vegan ice cream, if you like.

For a sure-fire celebratory dessert, look no further than this comforting classic with its soft, sticky sponge and dark, glossy toffee sauce, but here it's spiked with sweet, spicy stem ginger for extra festive pizzazz.

Sticky Stem Ginger Toffee Pudding

SERVES 9

Sponge
200 g (7 oz) dates, pitted
    and roughly chopped
1 teaspoon bicarbonate
    of soda
200 ml (7 fl oz) boiling water
75 g (3 oz) vegan butter,
    softened
2 tablespoons stem ginger
    syrup
50 g (2 oz) soft dark
    brown sugar
2 tablespoons flaxseed,
    soaked in 6 tablespoons
    water for 10 minutes
    to activate
1 teaspoon vanilla extract
75 g (3 oz) stem ginger,
    roughly chopped
150 g (5 oz) plain flour
2 teaspoons baking powder
½ teaspoon salt
½ teaspoon ground ginger

For the sponge, put the dates and bicarbonate of soda into a small heatproof bowl, pour over the measured boiling water and stir well, then set aside for 10 minutes.

Preheat the oven to 180°C (350°F), Gas Mark 4. Line a 23 cm (9 inch) square ovenproof dish or baking tin with nonstick baking paper.

Beat together the vegan butter, stem ginger syrup and brown sugar in a stand mixer or in a large bowl with an electric hand whisk or a wooden spoon until pale and fluffy. Fold in the activated flaxseed solution, vanilla extract, stem ginger and the soaked dates.

In a separate bowl, whisk together the flour, baking powder, salt and ground ginger, then fold into the vegan butter mixture until just combined.

Pour the batter into the lined tin and smooth the surface with a spatula, then bake for 30–35 minutes, or until the sponge is springy to touch.

recipe continues overleaf

Sauce
300 g (10 oz) soft dark
    brown sugar
1 tablespoon stem ginger
    syrup
200 g (7 oz) coconut cream,
    plus extra (optional),
    to serve
150 g (5 oz) vegan butter
½ teaspoon salt
1 teaspoon vanilla extract

Meanwhile, make the sauce. Mix together all the ingredients, except the vanilla extract, in a heavy-based saucepan and heat over a medium heat until bubbling and thick, stirring occasionally. Remove from the heat and stir in the vanilla.

Once the sponge is cooked, remove from the oven, cut into 9 squares and serve in bowls with the warm toffee sauce poured over, along with extra coconut cream if you like.

Mincemeat and sweet spiced apples make the perfect pairing for a seasonal strudel. It's an impressive dessert but an easy one to whip up.

Mincemeat & Apple Strudel

SERVES 8

625 g (1¼ lb) Bramley apples, peeled, cored and cut into roughly 1 cm (½ inch) chunks
2 tablespoons soft light brown sugar
1 teaspoon ground cinnamon
¼ teaspoon ground nutmeg
¼ teaspoon ground ginger
finely grated zest of 1 lemon
250 g (8 oz) vegan mincemeat
50 g (2 oz) ground almonds
4 vegan filo pastry sheets, each about 48 × 25 cm (19 × 10 inches)
50 g (2 oz) vegan butter, melted
50 g (2 oz) flaked almonds

Glaze
50 g (2 oz) icing sugar
2 tablespoons lemon juice

Preheat the oven to 200°C (400°F), Gas Mark 6. Line a large baking tray with nonstick baking paper.

Mix together the apple chunks, brown sugar, spices and lemon zest in a large bowl, then stir in the mincemeat and ground almonds.

Place a filo pastry sheet on the lined tray and brush with some of the melted vegan butter. Top with another sheet of pastry and again brush with the butter, then repeat with the remaining 2 sheets.

Form the mincemeat and apple mixture into a log shape about 9 cm (3½ inches) wide lengthways in the centre of the layered filo, leaving at least a 7 cm (3 inch) clear border at either end. Fold in the short sides, then roll up the pastry tightly around the filling from one longer side to the opposite longer side until you have a giant spring roll-type shape, with the seam on the underside.

Brush all over with the remaining melted vegan butter, scatter over the flaked almonds and bake for 40–45 minutes until golden. Remove from the oven and let the strudel cool for 30 minutes or so.

Mix the icing sugar with the lemon juice in a bowl to make an opaque but viscous glaze. Using a spoon, drizzle the glaze over the strudel, then slice and serve.

A flourless oozy, gooey chocolate pudding when warm out of the oven, this turns almost brownie-like the next day when cold. So here you have two desserts in one – the gift that keeps on giving!

Chocolate Chestnut Pudding

SERVES 8

250 g (8 oz) vegan dark chocolate, broken into small chunks
225 g (7½ oz) vegan butter, plus extra for greasing
400 g (13 oz) chestnut purée
100 g (3½ oz) apple purée
50 g (2 oz) cocoa powder, plus extra for dusting
200 g (7 oz) soft light brown sugar
2 teaspoons vanilla extract
½ teaspoon salt
vegan cream or vegan ice cream, to serve (optional)

Preheat the oven to 200°C (400°F), Gas Mark 6. Grease a 20 cm (8 inch) dish.

Melt the chocolate along with the vegan butter in a heatproof bowl set over a pan of barely simmering water (make sure the bottom of the bowl isn't touching the water), stirring gradually until completely melted and combined. Remove from the heat.

In a separate bowl, whisk together the chestnut and apple purées, cocoa powder, brown sugar, vanilla extract and salt. Fold gently into the melted chocolate and butter.

Pour the batter into the prepared dish, smooth the surface with a spatula and bake for 45 minutes–1 hour, or until springy to the touch.

Remove from the oven and allow to cool slightly. Dust with cocoa powder before spooning out onto plates. Serve warm with vegan cream or vegan ice cream, if you like.

The combination of jam and rice pudding is a firm favourite, so here is a more sophisticated variation on that winning formula featuring vanilla and orange-flavoured sweet roasted plums for a suitably luxurious Christmas dessert.

Roasted Plums & Creamy Rice Pudding

SERVES 4–6

Roasted plums
8 ripe plums, stoned and quartered
100 g (3½ oz) caster sugar
½ vanilla pod, split lengthways and seeds scraped out, pod reserved (reserve remaining ½ vanilla pod for the rice pudding – see below)
finely grated zest and juice of 1 orange

Rice pudding
150 g (5 oz) pudding rice
75 g (3 oz) caster sugar
½ vanilla pod, split lengthways and seeds scraped out, pod reserved (see above)
400 ml (14 fl oz) can coconut milk
300 ml (½ pint) oat or almond milk
a few gratings of nutmeg
pinch of salt

Preheat the oven to 190°C (375°F), Gas Mark 5.

Place the plum quarters in a medium-sized ovenproof dish and sprinkle over the sugar, vanilla pod half and seeds and orange zest and juice. Cover with foil and roast for about 20 minutes.

Take off the foil and roast for another 20 minutes. Remove from the oven and set aside, discarding the vanilla pod half.

Mix together the rice pudding ingredients in a medium-sized saucepan and cook over a low heat for around 30 minutes, stirring regularly, until the rice is cooked and the milk thickens and becomes creamy.

Remove the vanilla pod half and serve the rice pudding in bowls with a generous spoonful of roasted plums along with a drizzle of the syrup residue from the roasting dish.

As if panettone isn't delicious enough on its own, smothered in marmalade, soaked in creamy custard and baked with a crunchy sugar topping it is elevated to a showstopper dessert. It's just as good served with vegan ice cream as an alternative to the vegan cream.

Panettone Marmalade Bread Pudding

SERVES 6

300 g (10 oz) vegan panettone, cut into thick slices
100 g (3½ oz) vegan butter
100 g (3½ oz) marmalade
1 heaped tablespoon cornflour
500 ml (17 fl oz) almond milk
100 g (3½ oz) vegan cream, plus extra to serve
2 tablespoons caster sugar
1 teaspoon vanilla extract
finely grated zest of ½ orange
2 tablespoons demerara sugar

Preheat the oven to 180°C (350°F), Gas Mark 4.

Lay the slices of panettone out on a baking tray and toast for 10 minutes. Remove from the oven and let the panettone cool, then generously spread with the vegan butter and top with the marmalade. Arrange the panettone slices in a medium-sized ovenproof dish.

Mix the cornflour with a little of the almond milk in a small bowl to make a smooth paste. Heat the rest of the almond milk with the vegan cream, caster sugar and vanilla extract in a medium-sized saucepan until just below boiling point. Stir in the cornflour paste and cook, stirring constantly, until the custard thickens. Stir in the orange zest.

Pour the custard over the panettone slices, pushing them slightly down so that they are submerged and nicely soaked in the custard. Sprinkle over the demerara sugar and bake for 40 minutes. Remove from the oven, cut into slabs and serve warm with extra vegan cream.

Aquafaba meringue made with brown sugar gives it an almost caramel-like flavour, which works so well with bright, sharp blood oranges and softly whipped cream.

Blood Orange Pavlova

SERVES 6–8

125 ml (4 fl oz) aquafaba
½ teaspoon white vinegar
200 g (7 oz) soft light brown sugar
4 blood oranges, or regular oranges or clementines if you can't find any
3 tablespoons caster sugar
400 g (13 oz) can coconut whipping cream
5–7 physalis, to decorate (optional)

Preheat the oven to 140°C (275°F), Gas Mark 1. Line a large baking tray with nonstick baking paper.

Whisk the aquafaba with the vinegar in a stand mixer or in a thoroughly clean, large, preferably metal bowl with an electric hand whisk on a high speed for about 8–10 minutes, or until the mixture holds stiff peaks.

Whisk in the brown sugar gradually, a tablespoon at a time, until the meringue is fluffy, stiff and pale brown in colour.

Carefully spoon the meringue on to the lined tray into a circle roughly 23 cm (9 inches) in diameter. Bake for about 2 hours, or until the meringue is set and comes away from the lining paper easily.

Meanwhile, cut the peel and pith off the oranges, then slice the fruit widthways into 1 cm (½ inch) thick rounds. Place in a bowl, scatter over 1 tablespoon of the caster sugar and set aside to macerate.

Once the meringue is ready, remove from the oven and let it cool completely. Then whip the coconut whipping cream with the remaining 2 tablespoons caster sugar in a large bowl until it holds soft peaks. Spoon on to the meringue and top with the orange slices and physalis, if you like. Carefully slice and serve.

This is a great recipe to make with the kids – you can melt the chocolate and spread it out, then have the various different topping and flavouring options ready for them to choose from and decorate the chocolate with. It makes great Christmas gifts too.

Chocolate Bark

400 g (13 oz) vegan
  chocolate, dark, dairy-free
  milk or a mixture of both,
  broken into small chunks

*Optional flavourings/
  toppings*
¾ teaspoon peppermint or
  orange extract
toasted nuts, roughly
  chopped
seeds
dried fruit, larger ones
  roughly chopped
candy canes, broken into
  small pieces
crystallized ginger, roughly
  chopped
vegan marshmallows, cut
  into small pieces
popcorn
sea salt flakes

Line a large baking tray with nonstick baking paper.

Melt the chocolate in a heatproof bowl set over a pan of barely simmering water (make sure the bottom of the bowl isn't touching the water), stirring gradually until completely melted. Remove from the heat.

If you are flavouring your chocolate with peppermint or orange extract, stir it in now.

Pour the melted chocolate on to the lined tray and use a spatula to spread it out until about 5 mm (¼ inch) thick. Scatter over the chosen toppings and then place in a cool area of the kitchen for at least 1 hour until the chocolate has set completely. You can refrigerate it to speed up the setting process.

Once completely set, break into rough shards. It can be stored in an airtight container for up to 2 weeks.

Sweet cranberries spiked with orange zest in a flaky icy form make a very refreshing and palate-cleansing end to a rich festive meal. The granita can be made several days in advance and stored in the freezer.

Cranberry Granita

500 ml (17 fl oz) water
500 g (1 lb) fresh or frozen
  cranberries
350 g (11½ oz) caster sugar
finely grated zest and juice
  of 2 oranges

Mix together all the ingredients in a medium-sized saucepan and cook over a medium heat until the sugar dissolves and the cranberries begin to burst. Set aside to cool completely.

Blitz the cooled cranberry mixture in a blender until puréed, then strain through a sieve into a freezer-safe container with a lid. Seal the container and freeze for 2 hours.

Remove from the freezer and scrape the frozen mixture with a fork until broken up. Reseal and return to the freezer for another hour, then again break up the mixture with a fork. Repeat this process every hour for 5 hours until the whole mixture is uniformly flaky and icy. Keep in the freezer until ready to serve, then spoon into glass dishes or glasses.

Index

Glossary

UK	US
Apple purée	Applesauce
Aubergine	Eggplant
Baking beans	Pie weights
Baking paper	Parchment paper
Beans, butter	Beans, lima
Beetroot	Beets
Bicarbonate of soda	Baking soda
Cavolo nero	Tuscan or black leaf kale
Celeriac	Celery root
Chilli flakes	Dried red pepper flakes
Clingfilm	Plastic wrap
Coriander	If referring to the leaves, cilantro
Cornflour	Cornstarch
Courgette	Zucchini
Flour, plain	Flour, all-purpose
Flour, strong white	Flour, white bread
Ginger, stem	Ginger, preserved
Grill	Broil/broiler
Jug	Liquid measuring cup or pitcher
Kitchen paper	Paper towels
Lentils, Puy	Lentils, French green
Loaf tin, 1 kg (2 lb)	Loaf pan, 9 × 5 × 3 inches
Mushrooms, chestnut	Mushrooms, cremini
Oats, porridge	Oats, rolled

UK	US
Pastry case	Pastry shell or crust
Polenta	Cornmeal
Potatoes, King Edwards or Maris Piper	Potatoes, russet or Yukon Gold
Pudding basin	Deep, ovenproof glass or ceramic bowl
Pudding rice	Short-grain white rice
Rocket	Arugula
Spring onions	Scallions
Stone, avocado/plum	Pit, avocado/plum
Sugar, caster	Sugar, superfine
Sugar, icing	Sugar, confectioners'
Sultanas	Golden raisins
Swede	Rutabaga
Sweetcorn	Corn kernels
Tea towel	Dish towel
Tomato purée	Tomato paste
Treacle	Molasses
Whisk, electric hand	Mixer, electric handheld
Wholemeal	Whole-wheat
Yeast, fast-action dried	Yeast, active dry

hamlyn

First published in Great Britain in 2023 by
Hamlyn,
an imprint of Octopus Publishing Group Ltd,
Carmelite House
50 Victoria Embankment
London EC4Y 0DZ
www.octopusbooks.co.uk

An Hachette UK Company
www.hachette.co.uk

Photography copyright © Octopus Publishing
Group 2023
Text copyright © Octopus Publishing Group 2023
Design and layout copyright © Octopus Publishing
Group 2023

Distributed in the US by
Hachette Book Group
1290 Avenue of the Americas
4th and 5th Floors
New York, NY 10104

Distributed in Canada by
Canadian Manda Group
664 Annette St.
Toronto, Ontario, Canada M6S 2C8

All rights reserved. No part of this work may
be reproduced or utilized in any form or by any
means, electronic or mechanical, including
photocopying, recording or by any information
storage and retrieval system, without the prior
written permission of the publisher.

ISBN 978-0-600-63803-2

A CIP catalogue record for this book is available
from the British Library.

Printed and bound in China

10 9 8 7 6 5 4 3 2 1

Editorial Director: Natalie Bradley
Editor: Sarah Allen
Copy Editor: Jo Richardson
Art Director: Jaz Bahra
Photographer: Charlotte Nott-Macaire
Props Stylist: Davina Perkins
Food Stylist: Sam Dixon
Assistant Production Managers: Lucy Carter
and Nic Jones

Standard level spoon measurements are used
in all recipes.
1 tablespoon = one 15 ml (1/2 fl oz) spoon
1 teaspoon = one 5 ml (1/6 fl oz) spoon
Both imperial and metric measurements
have been given in all recipes. Use one set of
measurements only and not a mixture of both.

Merry
Christmas
& a Happy
New Year!